OUR CHURCH

Its LIFE

and MISSION

The Story of the

Wisconsin Evangelical Lutheran Synod

(A revision of YOU AND YOUR SYNOD)

Revised by Elmer C. Kiessling

NORTHWESTERN PUBLISHING HOUSE

Milwaukee, Wisconsin

On December 11, 1981, Prof. emer. Elmer C. Kiessling entered his eternal rest before this revision could be produced. This volume, therefore, is a fitting memorial to him for the years he spent serving the Lord in our church.

Thanks are due also to the several persons who helped bring the information in the revision up to date for publishing now.

The Editor

Photo of Dove on front cover by Dave Sherwin

The cover photo of the earth from outer space, courtesy of the National Aeronautics and Space Administration.
Used by permission.

The maps, "WISCONSIN SYNOD-1989" and "MIDWESTERN WELS-1989," designed and prepared by Dr. John C. Lawrenz

Produced by the Board for Parish Education
Wisconsin Evangelical Lutheran Synod

Northwestern Publishing House
1250 N. 113th St., P.O. Box 26975, Milwaukee, WI 53226-0975
© 1990 by Northwestern Publishing House. All rights reserved
Published 1990
Printed in the United States of America
ISBN 0-8100-0320-1

OUR CHURCH: ITS LIFE AND MISSION

Contents

PREFACE

Our Church: Its Life and Mission is the third revision of a book originally written by the late Professor E. E. Kowalke and published under the title *Our Synod and Its Work*. In the present revision more attention has been given to the story of the founders and the gradual change from their conciliatory to our present confessional Lutheranism.

Actually the Wisconsin Synod, even in its early unionistic period, has always been guided by a single purpose: to win as many souls as possible for Christ and to strengthen the faith of those who already believe in him. In the steadfast pursuit of this purpose, our synod has grown to be a body of more than 315,000 confirmed and more than 415,000 baptized members.

It has fostered Christian education at all levels—from kindergarten and the grades, through high school and college, to graduate work at its seminary. Our synod has carried the gospel into all fifty states through its home missions and to five continents through its world missions. Though repudiating the "social gospel," it has been mindful of the less fortunate and the "scattered people" and has created special ministries to serve their needs. To further these activities, our church has developed an administrative system that is comprehensive and competent.

All these synodical endeavors are presented and described in *Our Church: Its Life and Mission*. The book should appeal to members who want to know more about the great cause in which they are partners and helpers; to pastors and church leaders as an aid in their activities with youth groups, men's clubs, ladies' organizations, stewardship personnel and Bible classes; to teachers in Lutheran elementary schools who should find it a useful tool in acquainting their pupils with the history of our church and the scope of its mission. It may even awaken in some of the young people a desire to serve our synod as future pastors, teachers or lay leaders.

A reading of our synod's history will show, above all, that the Lord's blessing has rested upon our church's endeavors the past 140 years. There have been setbacks, crises, times of frustration, but none so crucial or discouraging that we cannot take comfort from the action of the Prophet Samuel. After Israel had emerged victorious from a desperate battle with the Philistines, "Samuel took a stone and set it up between Mizpah and Shen. He named it Ebenezer, saying, 'Thus far has the Lord helped us' " (1 Samuel 7:12).

Unit One
BEGINNINGS OF OUR CHURCH

CHAPTERS

1. Wisconsin, a Land of Opportunity
2. Immigrants
3. Roots of Our Church
4. Birth of Our Church

Chapter 1

WISCONSIN, A LAND OF OPPORTUNITY

What Pioneers Found

As we look about us anywhere in Michigan, Wisconsin or Minnesota today, it is hard to realize that only a century and a half ago these home states of our church or synod were a wilderness. Much of this land was covered with primeval forests—"fair ranks of trees . . . massy and tall and dark," as William Cullen Bryant describes them in his *Forest Hymn*.

Before 1830 there were almost no white people living in this vast territory, except in a few forts and small military posts in Detroit, in Mackinac at the head of Lake Michigan, in Green Bay, Portage, Prairie du Chien, and at Fort Snelling near present-day St. Paul.

Wisconsin was opened for settlement in 1836, but a traveler who made the journey from Fort Winnebago at Portage to Fort Howard at Green Bay in 1837 reported that there was not one house between Portage and Fond du Lac (59 miles) and only one house between Fond du Lac and Green Bay (61 miles). There were, of course, no roads in those days, and even the Military Road from Green Bay to Prairie du Chien, which was opened in 1838, was hardly more than a trail through the woods. It was difficult to follow even with the help of occasional markers. When an early settler wrote home to his parents in Europe that this country was "woods, woods, woods, as far as the world extends," he was giving an accurate picture of the whole area.

Michigan had enough white inhabitants to be declared a state as early as 1837. Wisconsin was admitted to the Union eleven years later, in 1848. Minnesota, organized as a territory in 1849—one year before our synod was founded in Milwaukee—achieved statehood in 1858.

Indians were still numerous in all three states. The first short-lived Lutheran synod in Michigan was called the "Mission Synod" because the three pastors who founded it expected to do missionary work among the Indians. In Wisconsin the tragic Blackhawk

War of 1832 brought an end to troubles with Indians. Yet decades passed before the various tribes were either moved across the Mississippi or confined to reservations. Pioneer women and children never ceased to be afraid when an Indian suddenly appeared out of the woods and walked up to their log huts, asking for flour and bread. There were occasional Indian scares, as in Watertown one day in 1862 when a rumor spread like wildfire that a band of "murderous red

men" was advancing upon the city. Presently a troop of citizens, "bearing guns, swords, pitchforks, scythes and spears," was marching northward, ready to sell their lives dearly. It soon became apparent that they had been the victims of a false alarm. No one ever found out how the rumor started, but it was probably the result of pent-up emotions created by bad news from the Civil War fronts and the report of a very real massacre at New Ulm during an uprising of the warlike Minnesota Sioux.

Wisconsin in 1850

The trickle of white settlers into Wisconsin territory became a fairly strong stream after 1836. The first boatload of Germans arrived in Milwaukee in 1839. The census of 1840 revealed a population of 30,945 in Wisconsin. By 1850, the year our church or synod held its first convention, the state's population had grown sixfold to 194,079, of whom 110,477 had been born in Europe. Milwaukee was then a city of 20,000 inhabitants. Watertown and Racine were next with about 4,000 each; then came Beloit, Janesville, Green Bay, Oshkosh, Fond du Lac and Beaver Dam.

It is surprising that these cities had grown as they did in about fifteen years, because the only way of reaching them was by boat, on foot or horseback, or by oxcart. Besides the Military Road from Green Bay to Prairie du Chien, there was another trail from Green Bay south through Manitowoc and Milwaukee to Chicago. Travel over these trails even in dry weather was slow and difficult. After spring thaws or heavy showers they often became impassable.

The best road in the state was the Plank Road, which had been built from Milwaukee to Watertown (45 miles) between 1848 and 1853 at a cost of $119,000. It was made of oak planks two inches thick and eight feet long and laid side by side on heavy oak stringers. The road was a luxury in its day, but after four years the planks were badly rotted. It was not repaired because by that time railroads provided cheaper and better transportation.

In 1850 there was just one-half mile of railroad in all of Wisconsin. That was the beginning of the line from Milwaukee to Waukesha. Ten years later it was possible to reach Janesville, Watertown, Madison, Prairie du Chien, La Crosse and Fond du Lac by rail. In 1850 the telegraph had been in use for six years, but the telephone remained unthought of for another twenty-five years. The first electric light was tried out in New York in 1880, but even kerosene lamps were unknown in 1850.

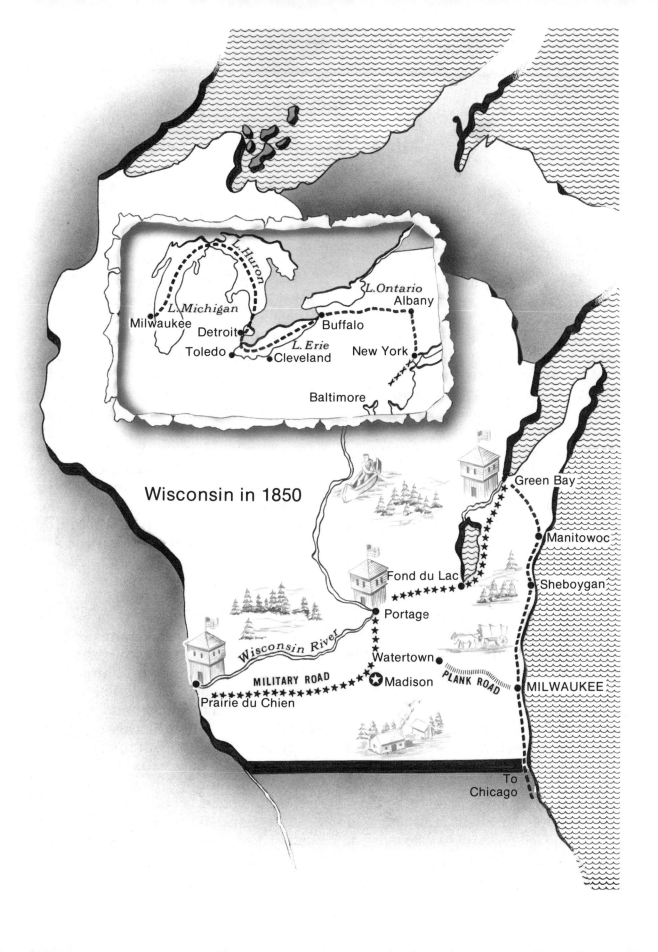

Wisconsin in 1850

L. Huron
L. Michigan
Milwaukee
Detroit
Toledo
Cleveland
L. Erie
L. Ontario
Albany
Buffalo
New York
Baltimore

Green Bay
Manitowoc
Sheboygan
Fond du Lac
Portage
Wisconsin River
Watertown
MILITARY ROAD
Madison
PLANK ROAD
MILWAUKEE
Prairie du Chien
To Chicago

Chapter 2

IMMIGRANTS

Why They Came

Settlers from Germany, Switzerland and Norway kept pouring into Wisconsin, and among them were many Lutherans. Whatever disadvantages existed in the pioneer state, they were small when compared with those in Europe. Germany especially was overcrowded and burdened with a class system and oppressive laws that weighed heavily on the common people. There had been an attempt to throw off this yoke in the Revolution in 1848, but it failed miserably. The ringleaders were hunted down by the authorities and had to flee the country to save their lives. Many emigrated to Wisconsin, where they became known as "Forty-Eighters."

Under these conditions the masses of Germany listened eagerly to reports of a land of promise across the ocean. This land had climate and fertile soil like that of the fatherland, an abundance of fish and game, and a wonderful new element — freedom — that was almost unknown in the old country. In this "golden land" they would be free to choose whatever vocation they desired, free to prosper and provide for their families, and above all free to worship God according to their own consciences.

Ordeal of the Journey

Eventually the immigrants did find all these things, but they had to undergo tremendous hardships before enjoying them. The long ocean voyage was an ordeal. Fare on a sailing vessel amounted to only forty or fifty dollars a person, but passengers had to provide their own bedding and enough food for a trip that took anywhere from four to six weeks. The ships were small, unheated, crowded, and there were many sad gatherings at the ship's rail while a brief funeral service was read over a body that would find its rest in the waters of the Atlantic.

If the ocean voyage was hard, the overland trip to Wisconsin was often harder. The first lap out of New York or Baltimore could be made by railroad; the second, on a canal boat to Buffalo, took seven days during which time the traveler never changed his clothes and slept on the open deck. From Buffalo to Detroit and Milwaukee the trip was made either by steamboat or sailboat, depending on which happened to be available and the amount of money the traveler could afford to spend for his fare.

After landing in Milwaukee, Wisconsin, the newcomers traveled inland or north along the shore of Lake

Canal boat

Michigan, following directions sent by relatives and friends already in this country. Finding them was not always easy, since there was no such thing as an address. The immigrants might be dropped on the shore of Lake Michigan at Milwaukee, with all their possessions on the sand, a thunderstorm threatening, and thirty-five miles still separating them from relatives, who, they had been told, live somewhere in the woods near a place called Ixonia. Somehow most of the immigrants managed, with a little help and great deal of trouble, to find their acquaintances and establish their claims to a piece of land. The next task was to fell enough trees for a log cabin home and to begin the backbreaking toil of clearing the land and preparing the soil for the first crops.

Life on the Frontier

Getting used to the life on the frontier was made easier for many because people from the same churches and provinces of the old country tended to cling together and settle in the same sections in this new land. Thus in Wisconsin, Sheboygan and Manitowoc had large groups of Lutheran Mecklenburgers; Jefferson and Helenville, of Lutheran Bavarians and Swabians. A colony of Swabians had also found a home in east central Michigan. Areas around New Glarus and Monroe, Wisconsin, were solidly Swiss and others near Stoughton and Koshkonong, Wisconsin, just as solidly Norwegian. The Swiss were of the Reformed faith, while the Norwegians were Lutheran. There was even a settlement of Icelanders on Washington Island off the top of Door County in Wisconsin and of Lutheran Finns in Michigan's Upper Peninsula. All churches and provinces were represented in Milwaukee.

In spite of the rigors of pioneer life immigrants in their letters home spoke so enthusiastically about their new country that others decided to pack up their belongings and start for America. There were cases where almost all the inhabitants of a village put their money and resources into the hands of a treasurer and left home in a body. In 1849 John Kerler, an innkeeper and brewer in Memmingen, Bavaria, and a staunch Lutheran, became disgusted with political conditions in Germany after the aborted Revolution of 1848. He sent his son, another John, to scout the Midwest for a desirable place to settle. After a careful search young John recommended the area west and southwest of Milwaukee near the Plank Road. As a result of his glowing reports the Kerler family, their in-laws — the Franks — and a cluster of relatives came to America, some staying in Michigan but most settling in the Milwaukee area. They became prominent members of WELS congregations in Milwaukee and Racine, Wisconsin, and in Bay City and Saginaw, Michigan, and kept in touch with each other in a lively series of letters that were published in English translation.

Freedom of religion meant a great deal to Lutheran settlers in Wisconsin, Michigan and Minnesota. But in the first years of the great migration it more often resembled freedom **from** religion. In the forest wilderness of this new land there certainly was no persecution by the state, and no preachers in Lutheran churches proclaimed the doctrines of rationalism, as some were doing in Germany. Here there were hardly any Lutheran churches at all and only a few preachers, mostly of different faiths or doubtful morals. The words of Jesus, "They were harassed and helpless, like sheep without a shepherd" (Matthew 9:36), exactly described the situation as it existed among Lutherans in the years before our church came into being. To the founding fathers, the three states, Wisconsin especially, were a vast mission field "ripe for harvest."

Chapter 3

ROOTS OF OUR CHURCH

Langenberg Mission Society

If we search for the roots of a Christian congregation or a synod, we will be led back through the years into the distant past, until we finally arrive at the cross of Christ. Even that is not the beginning. Our search would not end until we arrived in the Garden of Eden, where God promised that he would send a Savior who would crush the head of the serpent and save sinful man. So a Christian congregation or synod has its ultimate roots in the cross of Christ and God's gracious promise of salvation.

But any organization composed of human beings also has historical roots nearer to them in space and time. Those of our church or synod take us first into the neighborhood of Milwaukee nearly a century and a half ago, then east to New York state, across the ocean to Germany, and finally to three small towns in the lower valley of the Rhine River.

The people now living in the three German towns of Langenberg, Elberfeld and Barmen have perhaps never even heard of the Wisconsin Synod, but in the 1820s a few Christians in those towns became interested in the spiritual welfare of the Germans who were emigrating in such large num-

bers to the United States. They formed a group that came to be known as the Langenberg Mission Society and established at Barmen a practical seminary to train missionaries.

The Langenbergers were part of a larger movement that arose among serious Christians in various cities of Germany and Switzerland, notably at Berlin, Basel and Hermannsburg. In-

Synod's German roots

spired by the command of Christ to preach the good news to all creation, they formed societies to support missions on the home front and in foreign countries. Believers of all denominations were invited to join. Confessional differences, especially those differences between Lutherans and Reformed in the doctrine of the Lord's Supper, were toned down. "In these days," read one of their manifestos, "when the foundations of Christianity are being deliberately undermined, the Christian brothers of all confessions must hold together."

Eventually these societies supplied our youthful synod with more than forty pastors and professors, with generous gifts of money, and with books for a seminary library. But the first two men sent to America by the Langenberg Society in 1837 were destined for work in New York City. At that time there was probably not a single German Lutheran in Wisconsin.

John Muehlhaeuser: Early Years

One of these first two Langenberg representatives was John Muehlhaeuser (MEAL-hoyz-er), the "father" of the Wisconsin Synod. The story of how he came to be chosen by the society and how he happened to come to Wisconsin is an interesting one. It reveals a great deal about his own character and that of the organization which in its early years was popularly referred to as the "Muehlhaeuser Synod."

Born in 1803 in Wuerttemberg (Swabia), John Muehlhaeuser was brought up a Lutheran in an area where Lutherans, though in the majority, were tolerant toward members of the Reformed minority, freely admitting them to communion in Lutheran churches. As a journeyman baker young Muehlhaeuser came in contact with the head of the Basel Mission Society, Christian Spittler, who persuaded him to join his "Pilgrim Mission" and serve as a lay missionary in Roman Catholic Austria.

For three years Muehlhaeuser brought the testimony of the gospel to isolated Lutheran and Reformed Christians in Austria and Hungary.

John Muehlhaeuser

He supported himself at his trade, when he could, or as colporteur—a peddler of Bibles and religious literature. After suffering repeated harassments from the Catholic government, he was arrested, kept in prison for nine months and finally expelled from the country. During his imprisonment he was instrumental in converting two Jewish fellow prisoners, a prison guard, and one of the police officers who conducted him to the border. A diary which he kept throughout his "pilgrimage" was later given to our synod by his son Gottlob, a Missouri Synod pastor who had graduated from Northwestern College in 1874. The diary is preserved in the synod archives.

On his return from Austria, Muehlhaeuser enrolled at the Barmen Seminary and studied there for two years. He was already thirty-four—the same age as Luther at the beginning of the Reformation—when the society sent him overseas to establish a Christian school for German children in New York City. But parents in that area preferred to have their children attend public schools, where they could learn English. Muehlhaeuser's school folded, and he was urged to accept a call as a pastor to a church in Rochester, New York. Though he found it split by Reformed and Lutheran factions, he managed to keep the congregation together and to win the hearts of the people by his sincere preaching of the gospel and his "good-hearted, unselfish concern for others." He labored there for ten years—from 1838 to 1848—and married in 1842.

"Macedonian Call"

One day in 1846 Pastor Muehlhaeuser received a letter from the Langenberg Society announcing the forthcoming arrival of three young pastors. He was instructed to meet them in New York and take them under his wing. Steamships were already in operation then, making the ocean trip in two weeks and carrying most of the mail. But the three pastors came in a sailing ship. The journey took three times as long, but a Bremen shipping line offered free passage for Langenberg missionaries.

At any rate, Muehlhaeuser had ample time to travel to New York City to meet the trio. Two of the three, John Weinmann and William Wrede (RAY-day), were to become his dear friends and fellow founders of the Wisconsin Synod. Weinmann, like Muehlhaeuser, was a native of Swabia and an alumnus of the Barmen Seminary. Wrede had received his theological education elsewhere, but offered his services to Langenberg. A call from a church in Callicoon, about seventy-five miles northwest of New York City, was waiting for him, and he accepted it.

Weinmann, somewhat to his surprise, was directed to go to Wisconsin. Right after he left Germany, the Langenberg Society received a letter from a lay member of a struggling congregation in Oakwood township, south of Milwaukee, asking for a trustworthy pastor. The society immediately sent its instructions to New York—by steamship—designating Weinmann as the man to respond to the request.

The layman who had written the letter was a farmer named Ehrenfried Seebach. His impressive first name would one day be borne by his grandson, Ehrenfried Berg, late pastor and professor in our synod. In his letter Seebach informed the society that the Oakwood congregation of some 300 members had gone through a disillusioning experience when their pastor had to be dismissed because of scandalous conduct. Seebach had been asked to conduct reading services, and he had done so. "There is a great field here for Christian mission," he wrote, "and splendid congregations might soon, under a good shepherd, prosper and become mission centers for other localities; for there is a desire among a great many for the Word of God. But how shall they believe if it isn't preached to them?" This was truly a "Macedonian call." It not only brought Weinmann but Muehlhaeuser and Wrede to Wisconsin.

St. John's, Oakwood Rd., Oak Creek

Chapter 4

BIRTH OF OUR CHURCH

Founders Come to Wisconsin

John Weinmann proved to be a faithful, efficient and beloved pastor. He consolidated the straggling Oakwood flock. Known today as St. John Lutheran Church 10302 South 27th Street, Oak Creek, it is the oldest congregation of our synod. He also canvassed the whole region as far south as Racine, where he served another church. Weinmann sent regular reports of the bright mission prospects to his friend in Rochester, New York. Muehlhaeuser, who had some of the pioneer's blood in his veins, could not resist the western challenge. One day he decided to take up the wanderer's staff, as he had done nearly twenty years before in Austria. Resigning his charge, he applied to the New York Tract Society to be commissioned a colporteur, and in June 1848 he came to Milwaukee. For several months he trudged up and down streets of the city and roads of the adjoining country, bringing Christ's message with his Bibles and tracts to unchurched Lutherans and other Protestants. But the work was too rigorous for him, and he became ill.

It was then that two friends, a Presbyterian minister and a Congregational minister, advised him to form a congregation of his countrymen in Milwaukee. They offered to rent him a hall on the west side of the river, then known as Kilbourntown. Muehlhaeuser accepted their offer and formed an "evangelical" congregation, meaning that Reformed as well as Lutherans would be welcomed as members. Yet shortly afterward when the church was incorporated, the word Lutheran, possibly on Weinmann's advice, was added, and it became Grace Evangelical Lutheran Church. A few years later when Grace was ready to build its first house of worship, it moved from Kilbourntown, where there were already ten German churches of various denominations, to its present site on the east side of the river.

Grace Ev. Lutheran Church

Pastor Wrede evidently kept in touch with his western brothers, for in 1849 he followed them to Milwaukee and took charge of a congregation at Granville (now a part of Milwaukee on North 107th Street). The Granville Lutherans, like those of Oakwood, had been hoodwinked by a previous pastor. The man in this case was Paul Meiss, a former shoemaker, who though neither ordained nor licensed won the favor of the people, until he tried to foist a revival on them. He resigned after Wrede arrived, and the matter was cleared up.

The Oakwood and Granville troubles made it clear that not all men who offered their services could be sent out into the Wisconsin mission field without being examined beforehand. Some were dishonest, and others were quite ignorant of things they were expected to preach and teach. Even when a man was found to be sincere, it was often necessary to instruct him in Lutheran doctrine before he was ready to serve as pastor or teacher.

Birthday

The three friends—Muehlhaeuser, Weinmann and Wrede—undoubtedly discussed these matters in the summer and fall of 1849. They came to the conclusion that an organization was needed to set up standards of Lutheran doctrine and practice and to examine each candidate or to provide additional training for him before recommending him to the young congregations in the state. It was for this purpose that they met in the rented hall of Grace Church in Kilbourntown on December 8, 1849, to form the "First German Evangelical Lutheran Synod of Wisconsin."

They then proceeded to the election of officers. Muehlhaeuser, the oldest, was elected president; Weinmann, secretary; and Wrede, treasurer. It was the only time in our history that the roster of officers nearly coincided with the entire synod membership.

The next item on the agenda was to schedule the first regular convention of the "Synod of Wisconsin." The newly elected officials designated May

Salem Ev. Lutheran Church

26, 1850, as the date and Salem Church in Granville as the place of the meeting. President Muehlhaeuser was to prepare a constitution expressing their confessional position and to present it for discussion and acceptance. That ended the business of this first and memorable meeting held in our church.

In imagination we can picture the men as they emerged from the little hall, thoughtful but confident. God had been with them in a special sense on that day. He would surely sustain them in the great work ahead. It was in this hopeful mood that they said goodbye before returning to their homes. Muehlhaeuser, the only married man in the group, lived nearby. The younger men whose parishes lay in opposite corners of Milwaukee County, had a longer way to go, and they probably traveled on foot. Milwaukee had few if any means of transportation, and it is hardly likely that either of the pastors owned a horse, to say nothing of a horse and buggy. This was still the era in which a traveling missionary—and every pastor was a missionary at that time—had to make his way by walking, only occasionally riding a horse or being picked up by some farmer to ride in a wagon behind a team of horses or oxen.

Unit Two

GROWTH OF OUR CHURCH

CHAPTERS

Chapter 5

"MUEHLHAEUSER SYNOD"

First Convention

Though history is silent about what was going on in the newly formed organization during the five months before May 26, 1850, the interval must have been filled with missionary activities. When the synod convened in May, it was attended by five pastors, representing eighteen congregations.

President Muehlhaeuser 1850-1860

Of these Muehlhaeuser served two, Weinmann two, Wrede three, Kaspar Pluess—a new man—four, and the irrepressible Paul Meiss seven. Most of the new congregations were concentrated in areas around Slinger (then known as Schlesingerville), West Bend and Sheboygan. There seems to have been only one lay delegate; he was from Grace Church. Jacob Conrad, a colporteur for the American Tract Society, put in an appearance and expressed his desire to enter the ministry. He was turned over to Wrede for training.

Muehlhaeuser's constitution was adopted after being discussed point by point. It pledged each pastor and theological candidate to the "true word of the Bible, the Unaltered Augsburg Confession, and the rest of the Lutheran Confessions." An interesting requirement was that a candidate be acquainted with the original languages of the Bible. Since Wrede was the only one who may have had a knowledge of Greek and Hebrew, this paragraph was very likely inserted at his request. Thus the study of languages, which is so important in the education of our church's pastors, was instituted at the very beginning.

Some nine paragraphs in the constitution prescribed the steps to be followed in licensing prospective pastors. According to this system a promising candidate was placed in charge of a congregation, but required to continue his instruction during a probationary period of two years, usually under the supervision of a neighboring pastor. Then, after being examined and approved by a two-thirds vote of the pastors, he would be formally ordained and accepted as a member of the ministerium, the association of clergy which in those years was considered as important as the synod itself. The licensing system was discontinued in 1856. Yet in the early years it did help to alleviate the shortage of pastors, and one of the very reasons for founding the synod was to exercise some control over would-be ministers through the licentiate. Another resolution passed during the meeting was "that every preacher belonging to the synod shall concern himself especially with the youth, and conduct a day school, Bible hours, and mission classes." As a result nearly half the congregations had parochial schools by 1860.

Venerable President

Anniversaries of our church are usually dated from this first convention of 1850. Of the five charter members who launched it on its career, only Muehlhaeuser stayed with the organization. Weinmann soon accepted a call to Baltimore, Maryland. In 1858, while returning from a trip to Germany to visit his aged mother, he perished in the burning of the ship, *Austria*. A bungling crew, in carrying out the command of the captain to fumigate the steerage with tar smoke, upset a kettle of hot tar, which caught fire and enveloped the ship in flames. Only a few of the 600 passengers were saved. Wrede returned to Germany to serve a congregation there. We hear of him only once more when Muehlhaeuser, during a trip abroad in 1862, called on him and preached for him. Kaspar Pluess left the synod to join a Reformed classis (synod). Paul Meiss, zealous but unstable, was dismissed within a year by the West Bend congregation for dishonorable behavior. In the late 1850s he went to the South, where he died of yellow fever.

Fortunately other pastors were on hand to join the "Muehlhaeuser Synod." Jacob Conrad, after finishing his course of instruction under Wrede, was ordained and served ably in several congregations, the last one in Racine. W. Buehren, a former Methodist minister, and Daniel Huber, a former Catholic priest, were converted to Lutheranism and were accepted as members of the ministerium. This was also the time in which German societies began to send missionaries, many of them bearing names which became well-known in later synod history—Bading, Koehler, Reim, Goldammer, Brockmann, Hoenecke, Sauer, Albrecht, and those of two less-known men, Fachtmann and Moldehnke, our first two traveling missionaries.

During the middle years of the nineteenth century, the head of the Barmen Seminary and later of the Berlin Mission Society was Johann Christian Wallmann, a staunch Lutheran who imbued his students with a confessional spirit which was in direct contrast to the milder and more moderate Lutheranism taught at the Barmen Seminary while Muehlhaeuser studied there. Muehlhaeuser had no scruples about offering "every child of God and servant of Christ the hand of fellowship over the denominational fence." He did not hesitate to solicit gifts from Protestant well-wishers in the East for his new Grace Church or from the people of Milwaukee for the congregation's parochial school. Once he even belittled the emphasis on confessional writings as a reliance on "paper walls of partition."

The time came when the newcomers who had been trained by Wallmann or by confessional German Lutherans like Ludwig Harms considered such practices unionistic and raised the confessional walls and fences that were not to be crossed. But in the early 1850s these differences were not yet apparent. Almost all the pastors were younger men who had profited from the fatherly, pastoral concern and the practical wisdom and experience of their venerable president. They recognized and respected his "personal living faith, his childlike trust in the Savior, and his burning zeal to build the Lord's kingdom and to spend himself in the work." Disregarding the article in his own constitution that no pastor should be elected to the presidency for more than two consecutive terms of two years each, the younger pastors elected Muehlhaeuser again and again until 1860, when he refused the office because of the pressure of pastoral work and advancing age. His associates expressed their deep regret and created for him the office of "senior," with the privilege of being seated next to the president at all sessions. John Bading (BAH-ding) became the new president, and under him the "senior's" mild Lutheranism gradually gave way to a firmer stand on the Confessions.

President Bading 1860-1864, 1867-1889

Chapter 6

"WE MUST DIG A WELL IN OUR OWN COUNTRY"

Recruitment Problems

The synod report for 1860 listed twenty pastors serving forty-eight congregations, twenty-three parish schools and twenty Sunday schools. Are you amazed at the comparatively small number of pastors? The problem was not so much the lack of applicants as the winnowing of the applications to find suitable men. Muehlhaeuser's ties with the eastern synods of the Lutheran Church were still very close. The Eastern Pennsylvania Synod considered the Midwest one of its mission fields and regularly sent money and even men. Pastor John Heyer, founder of the Minnesota Synod, was sent by this Pennsylvania group. This synod also published in eastern church papers Muehlhaeuser's plea for pastors and offered to train students from Wisconsin in its seminary at Gettysburg, Pennsylvania. Only one young man, J. H. Sieker, availed himself of this opportunity. Some years after his graduation Sieker became pastor of a church in St. Paul, and later president of the Minnesota Synod. Before accepting a call to the oldest Lutheran church in America, St. Matthew of New York City, Sieker was instrumental in bringing about a closer relationship between the Minnesota and Wisconsin Synods.

Most of the responses to Muehlhaeuser's advertisements came from men of low caliber. One hopeful wanted free transportation to Wisconsin so that he could act as land agent for his relatives in connection with ministerial duties. Another requested a church at a high, well-drained locality in a quiet neighborhood with a comfortable salary. Muehlhaeuser gave him a piece of his mind and offered him a charge which met none of these conditions.

Out in the Mission Field

Out in the mission field our pastors often had to contend with both English and German Methodist preachers. There was a saying that Methodist circuit riders had gone west with the covered wagons, whereas the missionaries of certain other denominations waited until there were trains or even Pullmans. Certainly Methodists were very active on the frontier. Their insistence on emotional conversion and abstinence from alcoholic drinks, dancing, card playing and Sunday amusements appealed to some people and even won over a few Lutheran ministers.

31

who came from Racine every second week. Their next two ministers were disasters: the first an abrasive troublemaker, the second a rationalist, who taught that everything should be judged by reason rather than by the Word of God. In desperation the congregation placed an advertisement in several newspapers. They got a man from Chicago but had to dismiss him after two years. Finally, listening to better advice, they found a faithful shepherd in Christian Popp, who joined the Wisconsin Synod and served Friedens for many years.

In spite of problems like these the synod was growing, and the pastors, though few in number, were dedicated to the task of extending its boundaries. It was not unusual for a pastor to serve two to seven small neighboring

Congregations also suffered from intruders, usually men with a smattering of theology, glib tongues and pleasant personalities, who posed as pastors but were in fact hirelings. The example of the Lutherans in Kenosha, Wisconsin, who formed the nucleus of the later Friedens congregation, is hardly typical, but it shows what could happen. Their first pastor turned out to be a Methodist. Their second one, Daniel Huber, the converted former Catholic priest, was an honorable man but soon accepted a call to another parish. They were then served for a time by Pastor Weinmann, groups of Christians besides his home congregation, and in addition, to undertake an occasional missionary journey to a town or area still without a Lutheran church. In 1856 John Bading and Philip Koehler (KAY-ler) went on such an exploratory "hiking trip." It took them from West Bend to Algoma, Wisconsin, nearly ninety-five miles as the crow flies and led to the founding of several congregations. Moldehnke and Fachtmann carried the torch of the gospel to the towns of central Wisconsin and to the west as far as La Crosse. Fachtmann went from there to Minnesota, where he played a significant role in forming the Minnesota Synod. Trinity Church in Waukesha owed its existence to a quick canvass undertaken by Pastor Brockmann during an enforced four-hour layover in that city because of a missed train.

Still the demands of Lutheran settlers for spiritual care outran the supply of pastors. The leaders of our early church realized that more laborers were needed and that in the long run they could not depend on the German mission societies or eastern Lutheran synods but would have to train their clergy in a seminary of their own. President Bading admonished his colleagues in picturesque language: "We must dig a well in our own country, in our synod, from which the water flows." But the cost of a new seminary was far above the resources of the little synod.

Around 1860 negotiations were underway to conduct a theological seminary at Illinois State University, a Lutheran school in Springfield, maintained by three Illinois branches of the eastern General Synod. Nothing came of the project. Later, when the Missouri Synod acquired the university and turned it into a practical seminary with accelerated courses, many students from Wisconsin and Minnesota enrolled at the Springfield institution and received their ministerial training there.

Jubilee Trip

In 1862 our synod fathers decided to turn once more to Germany for help. In that year the Langenberg Society was observing the twenty-fifth anniversary of its organization. It was also the silver anniversary of the commissioning of John Muehlhaeuser, its first missionary to America. Muehlhaeuser gladly accepted the society's invitation to come to Germany to celebrate the double jubilee. The synod voted an extra $50 for their "senior's" travel expenses and instructed him to sound out the society about aid for a new seminary and to ask for the immediate commissioning of ten new pastors.

Muehlhaeuser's trip was crowned with success. He was able to visit his eighty-four-year-old mother and his former colleague Wrede and to win the approval of the Langenbergers for a new seminary. They promised money and also books for the library. The money was collected by President Bading during a fund raising journey among Lutheran churches in Germany and Russia the following year. It amounted to $10,000, a very handsome sum in those days. Bading fared equally well among the churches in Prussia, but the synod never received that money for reasons that will be given later.

When Muehlhaeuser returned from his jubilee trip, he brought four pastors with him. Among several who soon followed were John Brockmann, later pastor of St. Mark in Watertown, Wisconsin, and Adolf Hoenecke (HAY-ne-key), the future seminary president and professor of dogmatics (church doctrine).

Muehlhaeuser took an active part in the founding of the combined seminary and college in 1863, though he was deeply disappointed when it was located in Watertown rather than in Milwaukee. The influence of the new president, John Bading, pastor of St. Mark in Watertown, and of Adolf Hoenecke, newly arrived from Germany and pastor at Farmington near Watertown, was strong enough to sway the votes of ministers and delegates in favor of their hometown. Both Bading and Hoenecke soon moved to Milwaukee, Bading to become pastor at St. John and Hoenecke at St. Matthew. Had the calls to these Milwaukee congregations come a few years earlier, Northwestern College might today be situated in the heart of Milwaukee.

Interlude—
Two Brief Presidencies

When Pastor John Bading traveled to Europe in mid 1863 to collect funds for the proposed seminary, he was the president of the Wisconsin Synod. His term would not end until the 1864 synod convention. During his absence Gottfried Reim, pastor at Helenville, Wisconsin, served as acting president. President Bading's decision to remain longer in Europe than he had originally planned resulted in his absence at the 1864 synod convention.

At this convention, Pastor Gottlieb Reim was elected synod president in his own right, and Pastor William Streissguth, of St. John in Milwaukee, was elected vice president. After serving for nearly one year as president, Pastor Reim, for personal reasons, resigned his presidency just before the 1865 convention. Vice President Streissguth then served as acting president for one year. At the 1866 synod convention, William Streissguth was elected president and John Bading vice president. One year later, at the synod convention, President Streissguth resigned his presidency for health reasons, and John Bading once again was elected president of the Wisconsin Synod.

Chapter 7

AN ERA ENDS—A NEW ERA BEGINS

"His Charity Was Practical"

John Muehlhaeuser died at the age of sixty-four in 1867. His funeral was a civic event. Prominent Milwaukeeans were in attendance, and the whole police force was needed to escort the three-quarter-mile-long procession from Grace Church to the cemetery. Everyone agreed that "Milwaukee had never seen its like." The *Milwaukee Sentinel*, in a tribute to Muehlhaeuser, praised him as a public-spirited citizen and a self-sacrificing pastor and teacher. It was recalled that during the cholera epidemic of 1855, he had not, like many, fled the city, but fearlessly and with untiring devotion had taken care of the sick and dying, ministering to their bodily and spiritual needs. "He died poor," concluded the *Sentinel* writer, "a sufficient proof that his charity was practical." President Bading, in his presidential address at the next synod meeting, eulogized Muehlhaeuser as "the father, founder and intercessor of the synod, to whom next to the grace of God it owes its existence."

Muehlhaeuser's death marked the end of an era. To the end of his life he had worked hard to preserve friendly relations with the eastern Lutheran synods and the German mission so-

Dr. C. F. W. Walther

cieties, to whom "we are under great obligations." Just as strenuously he expressed his disapproval of the spirit of Missouri Synod "Old Lutherans," who "carried to extremes" their orthodoxy and their criticisms of the Wisconsin Synod. Dr. C. F. W. Walther, the famous Missouri theologian, had accused Muehlhaeuser and his associates of not being Lutheran because they were accepting aid from unionistic German societies and eastern synods.

Break with the German Mission Societies

There was some truth in Walther's criticism. The German societies were unionistic and expected our pastors to minister to Reformed as well as to Lutheran members. In a few of our congregations the two groups were almost equally divided, and trouble arose because they disagreed not only on the doctrine of the Lord's Supper but on the way it was distributed. Lutherans used wafers with the wine; the Reformed wanted plain bread. In one congregation the trouble became so severe that a committee of the synod tried to bring about peace by suggesting that both forms be used. A Lutheran pastor criticized this advice as contrary to the very nature of the sacrament, which ought to be an intimate communion between all those who partake of it. The synod then decided that only the Lutheran order of service would be followed in all its churches, even if it meant breaking with the German societies.

The break soon came. It was not easy to part with German friends who had done so much for us, and several pastors left the synod in protest over the action. Our church sent a dignified statement of its position to the Berlin Society and asked for the release of the money, amounting to over $7,000, that President Bading had collected in Prussia. The request was refused. The loss of this large sum caused a great deal of hardship, but our church never regretted its decision to take a forthright stand on the Lutheran Confessions and to reject unionism (altar and pulpit fellowship with those who do not agree with us in doctrine).

Fellowship with the Missouri Synod

For some time the conviction had been growing that the church which most truly represented pure Lutheranism and most resolutely refused to tolerate teachings that were out of harmony with the Bible was the Missouri Synod. Even our traveling missionary, Fachtmann, who was unionistically inclined, once reported that the "Old Lutherans" were "the salt of the society in which they are found," though he regretted their "unreasonably gruff" attitude. On the other hand, Dr. Walther admitted that if he had known how firmly our men were committed to the Lutheran Confessions, he would have urged a union long before. President Bading, in a conversation with several Missouri Synod pastors, found that "they desire peace as earnestly with us as we with them."

So it was that in 1868, the very year after Muehlhaeuser's death, the Missouri and Wisconsin Synods entered into doctrinal discussions that were to result in the forming of the Synodical Conference in 1872. From then on the two synods worked together and fought the battles of the church in oneness of spirit. They agreed to cooperate in the training of pastors.

Wisconsin placed its college in Watertown, Wisconsin, at the disposal of Missouri, and the latter reciprocated by inviting Wisconsin seminarians to study at its seminary in St. Louis, Missouri. For eight years, beginning in 1870, a number of Missouri Synod students attended Northwestern College, and Northwestern graduates and other Wisconsin Synod theological students received their education at Concordia Seminary.

Chapter 8

NEW LUTHERAN COLLEGE AND SEMINARY

Seminary Opens in 1863

In the meantime, in the early 1860s, much had happened in our church. The Civil War had cast its shadow over the whole nation, but it seems not to have affected the work of the church to any degree. The great achievement of the decade for our church was the founding of the seminary in Watertown. Actually it was intended to be a combination seminary, college and high school from the very beginning. Since high schools were almost unknown in Wisconsin in the 1860s, education for the ministry was to begin with boys who had hardly advanced beyond reading, writing and arithmetic in the one-room country schools. It was therefore necessary for the church to provide a preparatory school to equip students for work in its seminary.

The institution opened in September 1863 with three students and one professor, Dr. E. Moldehnke. The school was located in a private residence still standing on North Fourth Street in Watertown. A bronze marker was placed on the house at the time of the college centennial in 1965. Only one of the three students, A. F. Siegler, took the theological course. He left the seminary to study at St. Louis but returned to graduate. He served for years as a pastor in our church and became the ancestor of several generations of pastors.

"Kaffeemuehle"

Though the city of Watertown had redeemed its pledge to raise $2,000 for the institution if it were located there, money was so scarce that all hopes for the future of the school centered on the results of the collection that President Bading was then raising among Lutheran churches in Germany and Russia. When news arrived that his pleas for the little seminary in distant Wisconsin were attended with outstanding success, our church bought the first five acres of the present Northwestern College campus and broke ground in 1864 for its first building. The three-story edifice, topped by a small square cupola, was the most prominent landmark in Watertown for many years. Dedicated on September 14, 1865, it served as dormitory, classroom, dining hall and residence for the housekeeper and the dean of students. Because of its shape it was soon nicknamed the "Kaffeemuehle" (Coffee Mill). In the summer of 1894 it was struck by a bolt of lightning and destroyed by fire.

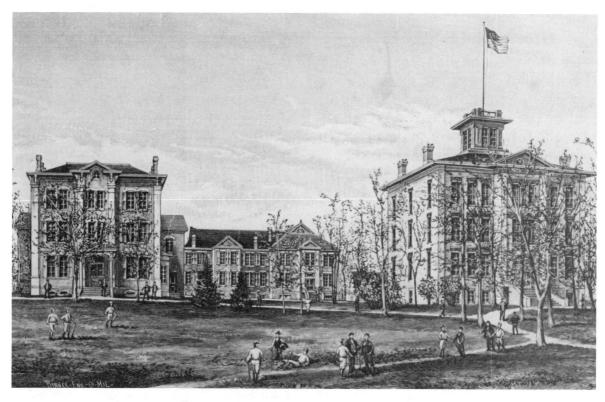

The "Kaffeemuehle" is the building to the right.

Soon after the dedication in 1865, this Lutheran school received its prestigious new name, "Northwestern University," which it kept until 1910. The seminary, which was a department of the university, graduated only twelve pastors in the seven years before its students transferred to Concordia Seminary in 1870. In this short time the seminary had already developed a distinctive Lutheran theology under its new professor, Adolf Hoenecke, who replaced Dr. Moldehnke, when the latter returned to Germany.

Gemeinde-Blatt

At this time the fathers of our church wisely decided to issue a church paper that would instruct the members of the congregations in doctrine and practice. They believed that a church paper would also help to increase in the members the feeling that they and other congregations of the synod belonged together because of their common faith and common problems. The first issue of this periodical, called the *Gemeinde-Blatt* (congregation paper), appeared September 1, 1865. As long as German was the common language in our congregations, the *Gemeinde-Blatt* served the church nobly. Although it was published for more than a century, until December 1969, its place as the official church paper had long before that been taken over by

39

The Northwestern Lutheran, which began publication in 1914.

Horse and Buggy Era

By the 1860s the pioneer age was on the way out. Traveling missionaries now rode on trains instead of going on foot or horseback. Dirt roads had replaced forest trails; rivers were bridged; the era of the horse and buggy was coming in. It would last until well into the present century. As late as 1915, St. Mark congregation in Watertown, Wisconsin, instructed its council "to have posts set at the church as soon as possible for tying horses of members who came in from the country." Rows of hitching posts, the parking places for horse-drawn vehicles, could be seen near every church in town and country.

Many pastors loved horses and had a fine steed and vehicle of their own. Others depended on the local livery stable, where a horse and buggy could be rented at any time for a modest fee. In these conveyances pastors called on parishioners, visited the sick, and, if they served a *filiale* (fee-lee-**ah**-le—affiliated congregation or preaching station), brought the gospel to the people there, usually at a late service or in the afternoon. In summer the members of these outlying congregations would be waiting outside the church doors until they spied their pastor's horse and rig in a rapidly moving swirl of dust in the distance. Pastors loved a horse that could keep a fast pace and bring them to the church on time. In the bitter cold winter, when roads were clogged with drifts, the pastor, wrapped in a buffalo robe, would arrive in a cutter—a light sleigh with a bowl-shaped body mounted on two slender runners. Before he left his *filiale*, he might instruct the children for an hour after the service or make a sick call at some lonely farmhouse. Life was slower-paced and more rigorous in those days. Yet pastors did not consider it a hard life. Theirs was the work to which the Lord had called them, and they did it gladly. They were in the King's service.

An American Lydia

Women are not often mentioned in connection with mission work in the early years of our church. Yet there is one example of a remarkable woman who gathered the first twenty families who formed the congregation at Winneconne, Wisconsin. In an unpublished paper, titled *Roots of Our Wisconsin Synod*, Pastor Armin Engel retold the inspiring story, which first appeared in two issues of the *Gemeinde-Blatt* in February 1915. It bears repeating.

Just before Christmas in the late 1860s a young couple came to the parsonage of Rev. William Streissguth, pastor of St. John Church in Milwaukee, to make arrangements for their marriage. The bridegroom, John Anderson, was a Norwegian Lutheran, who spoke German fluently. The bride, Marie, who had come to this country from Bavaria, admitted that she was a Roman Catholic. In the course of the conversation Pastor Streissguth remarked how nice it would be if they were of one faith and could attend the same church and partake of Holy Communion together.

Suddenly Marie turned to the pastor and asked, "How long would it take me to become a Lutheran?"

"You'd have to take instructions in the catechism," he replied. "If everything went well you could be confirmed by Easter."

"John, why don't we wait with our wedding until then?" Marie pleaded. "I want to become a Lutheran." John agreed somewhat reluctantly.

During the next months Marie, who worked as a housemaid on the east side of Milwaukee, came several times a week to be instructed. She was ready to be confirmed on Palm Sunday. Since she was already in her twenties and a rather large

woman, the pastor suggested that her confirmation be performed privately in the presence of the deacons. But Marie said, "I want to be confirmed with the children. I want to confess my faith publicly." And so she did. That same afternoon Marie and John were married, and not long afterward they moved to Winneconne.

Several years later William Streissguth, then a pastor in St. Paul, Minnesota, received a letter from Rev. Philip Brenner of Oshkosh, Wisconsin. "Do you remember Marie Anderson, the woman you confirmed?" Brenner asked. "She was unhappy without a church, so she canvassed the whole village of Winneconne and the surrounding neighborhood and gathered twenty Lutheran families who were willing to form a congregation. Then she asked me to serve them from Oshkosh. As a result of her work, we now have a thriving new congregation in the Wisconsin Synod."

Streissguth felt deeply gratified and, when some years later he happened to preach near Winneconne, he made it a point to call on the Andersons. He learned that Marie had had her share of grief, but that she had remained cheerful and steadfast in her Lutheran faith.

Many years then passed. Marie and John both died, but William Streissguth was still living as a retired pastor at the age of eighty-eight, when in January 1915 he read in the *Gemeinde-Blatt* that the Winneconne congregation had dedicated a beautiful new church. There was no mention of Marie in the accompanying historical sketch. Streissguth determined to remedy this omission. He wrote a lovely tribute to Marie, telling all he knew about her, and sent it to the *Gemeinde-Blatt*, where it appeared in the issue of February 5, 1915, under the heading, "An American Lydia."

But this was not the end of Marie's story. Another brief chapter appeared in the next issue of the paper. This one was written by Rev. Erdman Pankow, member of the first graduating class of Northwestern College and graduate of the seminary in St. Louis, Missouri. In 1875 he had been installed as the first resident pastor of the Winneconne-Bloomfield, parish and there he learned to know the Andersons. One day Marie told him the complete story of her conversion.

On her way to Sunday mass in Milwaukee before she knew John, she used to walk past Grace Lutheran Church. Rev. Theodore Jaeckel, Muehlhaeuser's successor, was pastor there at the time. One summer Sunday morning the door of the church was open, and she heard the voice of the pastor preaching the sermon. She paused at the doorstep for a minute but was soon so absorbed in what he said that she sat down and listened to the end. Here was something she had never heard before. She was impressed and also troubled, for she missed Sunday mass that morning and on several other Sunday mornings when she was tempted to sit in the rear of Grace Church listening to Pastor Jaeckel's preaching.

There followed a long struggle with her conscience, for she had been brought up to be a loyal Catholic. Hers was no sudden, light-hearted conversion, and it was not until she sat in Pastor Streissguth's study with her intended husband that she found the courage to do what her heart told her was the right thing to do. But it was on the doorstep of a church, wrote Pastor Pankow, rather than in a pastor's study that the Lord had first opened her heart to the gospel, as he had done to "a woman named Lydia, a dealer in purple cloth from the city of Thyatira" (Acts 16:14), many centuries ago.

Unit Three

TIES THAT BIND

"Make every effort to keep the unity of the Spirit through the bond of peace."—Ephesians 4:3

CHAPTERS

Chapter 9

THREE SYNODS JOIN WISCONSIN

Michigan Synod

In 1959 our segment of the Lutheran Church was renamed Wisconsin Evangelical Lutheran Synod. Up to that time our church was known as the Evangelical Lutheran Joint Synod of Wisconsin and Other States. This cumbersome name was adopted in 1892, when the three synods of Wisconsin, Minnesota and Michigan formed a federation. The long name was retained in 1917, when these synods and the Nebraska Synod merged into a single body.

Of the three federated synods of 1892, Michigan was the oldest, although it had been the last to affiliate with Wisconsin and the Synodical Conference. Its history goes back to 1831, when a company of Swabian Lutherans left their homes in Wuerttemberg and settled in the vicinity of Ann Arbor. In 1833 The Mission House of Basel, Switzerland, at their request, sent them an enthusiastic young pastor, Friedrich Schmid. He had begun his career as a blacksmith, following his father's occupation, and then switched to theology. In a few years Schmid had organized twenty small congregations and with two other Basel missionaries formed a Mission Synod, as the prelude to mis-

sionary work among the Indians. Several "Old Lutheran" pastors, hearing about the Indian mission and eager to take part in the project, came over from Germany and joined the synod.

But Schmid and his associates were plagued with troubles similar to those in Wisconsin. Basel expected them to minister not only to Lutherans but also to Reformed, and in Michigan the latter seem to have outnumbered the Lutherans. Schmid was somewhat more lenient in practice than his Wisconsin counterparts. When he accepted a Reformed minister as a member of his organization, the "Old Lutheran" pastors left in a body to join the Missouri Synod. That spelled the end of the first Michigan Synod.

Pastor Schmid continued his work as pastor and missionary, gathering congregations in southern Michigan and supplying them with pastors, mostly from his alma mater in Basel. By 1860 he was ready to make another attempt to form a synod. Eight pastors and three laymen responded to his invitation, founded the second Michigan Synod and elected him president. Among the pastors were two newcomers from Basel—Stephan Klingmann and Christoph Eberhardt, both of whom were later to serve as presidents of that synod. Eberhardt played a major role in guiding his colleagues in the troubled years ahead.

Christoph L. Eberhardt

In the late 1860s both the Wisconsin and Michigan Synods joined the General Council, an association of confessional Lutherans who were dissatisfied with the liberalism of the eastern General Synod. Wisconsin soon withdrew because the General Council could not make up its mind whether or not to tolerate altar and pulpit fellowship, lodges and millennialism— the widely held belief that Christ would return to reign visibly on earth for a thousand years before Judgment Day. Though the Michigan Synod took a stand against these so-called "four points," it stayed in the General Council for twenty years. Finally, tired of "acting as the conscience of the Council," it severed its connections and signified its willingness to federate with the Wisconsin Synod and join the Synodical Conference.

In 1885, under the prompting of Pastor Eberhardt, the Michigan Synod "dug its own well" by establishing Michigan Lutheran Seminary at Saginaw. By 1892 it had already supplied twelve pastors for Michigan congregations. But according to the terms of the federation, there was henceforth to be only one seminary in the Joint Synod, at Wauwatosa, Wisconsin. The Saginaw institution was to be reduced to the level of a preparatory school. This was a bitter pill for many of the Michigan pastors to swallow. Eberhardt died at this time, and that synod lost the benefit of his wise counsel. A distressing split developed. A minority of the clergy stayed with the Joint Synod, but the majority refused

Old Main of Michigan Lutheran Seminary

to have anything to do with the federation and continued to operate the Saginaw school as a seminary.

Fifteen years elapsed before the rift was healed. In 1910 all the dissidents agreed to return to the federation and accept its terms. Michigan Lutheran Seminary retained its name, but became the preparatory school that it still is today. In the years after 1910 Michigan men were in the forefront of the movement that led to the merging of the state synods into the Joint Synod of 1917.

Minnesota Synod

The first German Lutheran service in St. Paul, Minnesota, was conducted by itinerant Pastor F. W. Wier in 1855. But synod history in the North Star State did not begin until two years later, when a remarkable sixty-four-year-old man, Rev. Johann Christian Friedrich Heyer, walked down the gangplank of a Mississippi River steamboat docked at St. Paul. Behind Heyer lay twenty years of labor as home missionary for the Pennsylvania Ministerium and fourteen years as missionary in India. Before him lay a task as arduous as any he had known.

Here, as in Wisconsin, Methodist preachers had been the first on the scene and gathered an early harvest even among unchurched Lutherans. But Pastor Heyer was undaunted. He reorganized Wier's orphaned flock, canvassed St. Paul, preached in German and English as people desired, and often traveled sixty miles on foot to minister to isolated Lutherans who had requested his services. In the early summer of 1860 he and five other pastors founded the German Evangelical Lutheran Synod of Minnesota. Under Heyer and his successor in the presidency, G. Fachtmann—Wisconsin Synod's former traveling missionary—the Minnesota Synod enjoyed a remarkable growth. At Fachtmann's urging it joined the liberal, eastern General Synod. Confessional "Old Lutherans" of the membership resented this step toward unionism. Charges and countercharges between Fachtmann and these people, whom he had once characterized as "the salt of society" but "unreasonably gruff," became so bitter that he was finally ousted from the presidency and excommunicated. It was a sad end for the man who had performed yeoman's service in spreading the gospel in Wisconsin and Minnesota. Some years previously Pastor Heyer had left Minnesota and gone back to his mission in India. He retired at the age of seventy-eight and died in America two years later.

The new president of the Minnesota Synod was J. H. Sieker. He had received his theological education at Gettysburg Seminary of the General Synod but remained untainted by its unionistic spirit. Sieker's aim now was to bring about a closer relationship between the Wisconsin and Minnesota Synods. The latter severed its ties with the General Synod, and after lengthy discussions and prodding by Sieker and two Wisconsin men (Bading and Hoenecke), agreed to affiliate with Wisconsin. The Minnesota Synod was to have the privilege of training its future pastors at Northwestern University (now College) and to share in the editing, publishing and profits of the *Gemeinde-Blatt*. It was to call a professor of its own to serve at Northwestern and to contribute $500 annually for his support.

The newly established friendship received a jolt in 1875 when the Minnesota Synod asked for a delay on the payment of the $500. For two summers

in a row a plague of grasshoppers had desolated the state's harvest fields and impoverished its people. Besides, most of the synod's ministerial students were attending the seminary in Springfield, Illinois, rather than Northwestern. The Wisconsin Synod reacted to this communication "with the aplomb of Christian gentlemen," and their patience was rewarded. Minnesota stood shoulder to shoulder with Wisconsin in the controversies that

arose within the Synodical Conference, and its next presidents, Pastor A. Kuhn and C. J. Albrecht, helped to bring about the federation of the two synods in 1892.

One of the priorities of the federation was to reconstruct and unify the educational facilities of the member synods. This project, which called for the termination of the seminary in Saginaw, produced grief and dissension in Michigan. Exactly the opposite happened in Minnesota when it was learned that Dr. Martin Luther College, founded largely through the efforts of C. J. Albrecht in 1883, was to become the school for the training of teachers of the Joint Synod.

Ties between the Wisconsin and Minnesota Synods were also strengthened by their common work for the Apache mission, which the federation had opened in 1893. Both synods were ready to merge their identities and become districts in the new Joint Synod of 1917.

Nebraska—Flight from Synodical Ties

On May 23, 1866, a company of 125 Lutherans set out from Ixonia, Wisconsin, on a long trek to Nebraska. They traveled in fifty-three prairie schooners (covered wagons), each drawn by four oxen, and took with them a herd of cattle and a flock of sheep. It was a Lutheran congregation on the move, halting for divine service every Sunday morning. Nearly two months passed before they reached the land previously selected by a scouting party near the present

city of Norfolk. Their pastor, J. M. Heckendorf, joined them in the following year.

The trek to this distant frontier was as much a flight from Lutheran synods and synod squabbles as it was a quest for new land. Lutheran synods had greatly multiplied in the states east of the Mississippi River. It is only fair to say that in most cases these small groups were formed for the laudable purpose of testifying to a common faith and carrying on the Lord's work more effectively. But many became embroiled in disputes over points of doctrine and practice.

The area around Lebanon and Ixonia, Wisconsin, was especially hard hit in this respect. Pastors of the Missouri Synod disagreed with those of

the Buffalo Synod on the doctrine of the ministry. A Wisconsin Synod pastor became involved when he accepted members who had left a Missouri Synod congregation because its pastor insisted that each communicant come to him for private confession before partaking of the Lord's Supper. There were groups who thought it was wrong to lend money for interest and that taking out insurance betrayed a lack of faith in the Lord's promise to care for his people. Congregations split over cases of discipline. A Lebanon teacher named Pankow was excommunicated because he refused to admit that he had sinned in playing popular tunes on his violin in the church school after school hours. A large number of members followed

Pankow out of the church and established their own independent congregation, which Pankow served as pastor for decades.

Pankow and Heckendorf and their congregations were convinced that all this bickering resulted from the creation of synods, which inevitably lorded it over individuals and congregations. It was for this reason that the Ixonians moved to Nebraska, where they hoped to be unvexed by synod rules and officials. The plan worked very well for a while. Heckendorf trained his son to become his successor as pastor of an independent congregation, but the young man died shortly before the ordination ceremony, and the heartbroken father soon followed him in death. The moment of truth had come. Where would the congregation now find a pastor who was not already affiliated with a synod? Some of the members had heard that Professor Ernst of Northwestern University was waging a heroic fight back in Wisconsin against a project to unite all smaller synods into a larger —and presumably more powerful— state synod. Concluding that "Ernst must be one of us," they sought his counsel and even invited him to come to Nebraska. Ernst accepted the invitation and made the trip to Norfolk. To his surprise the elders of the church insisted on examining him for orthodoxy before they allowed him to occupy their pulpit. He soon removed all their doubts, and they gladly followed his recommendation to call a recent graduate of the seminary in Springfield, Illinois. He was Michael Pankow, son of the separatist teacher-pastor who had been the storm center in the Lebanon affair.

The Norfolk Lutherans still shunned affiliation with the Wisconsin Synod, but they did not object when their new minister joined that synod. A few years later they called a young Wisconsin Synod man, John Eiselmeier, to be the first teacher of their elementary school. Eiselmeier, had received his pedagogical training at Northwestern, which at that time still had a teachers' course. The Nebraskans worked together with the Wisconsin Synod in founding new congregations in their state and in carrying on mission work in Iowa, Colorado and South Dakota. The friendship deepened. In 1904 Nebraska became the fourth member in the federation of "Wisconsin and Other States," and ten years later it became the Nebraska District of the Joint Synod.

Chapter 10

DISTRICTS OF SYNOD

First Districts

In 1917 the federated Synods of Wisconsin, Minnesota, Michigan and Nebraska adopted a constitution that merged them into a single body, to which they transferred all their rights and properties. According to this agreement, Wisconsin was divided into three separate districts—the Northern Wisconsin District, which included the Upper Peninsula of Michigan, the Southeastern Wisconsin District and the Western Wisconsin District. Both of the latter extended into Illinois. Several Minnesota congregations in the Mississippi River valley were also added to the Western Wisconsin District. As districts, Minnesota, Nebraska and Michigan remained undivided, but all three included congregations and conferences beyond the borders of their states. For example, the Nebraska District included all of the states of Nebraska, Colorado, Wyoming, Utah and Kansas.

Pacific Northwest District

Soon after the merger, the Pacific Northwest and Dakota-Montana Districts were added to the Joint Synod. Pacific Northwest became a district in 1918 and Dakota-Montana in 1920. The history of these districts, both dating from the 1880s, is not a record of large numbers or rapid growth, but of building and maintaining congregation in outposts, where Lutherans represent only a small part of the total population.

The "cradle" of the Pacific Northwest was a home in Tacoma, Washington, where seven German Lutheran families gathered one day early in 1884 to discuss the possibilities of forming a congregation and calling a pastor. The group was successful in

St. Paul's Ev. Lutheran Church
Tacoma, Washington

obtaining a faithful shepherd in Pastor F. A. Wolf. Three days after he arrived in Tacoma, St. Paul Lutheran, the mother church of the district, was founded. St. Paul joined the Wisconsin Synod in 1898, and shortly after that the synod began sending missionaries, mostly young men, to the state of Washington. The work in this new field was strenuous. Pastor Fred Stern, for instance, served seven tiny congregations in towns that were fifty or more miles apart and could be reached only by stagecoach or horse and buggy. It took all week just to make the rounds. After a few years the young men usually accepted calls back to the Midwest. As a result there was often a scarcity of pastors. Today the district has congregations in Washington, Oregon, Idaho and Alaska.

Dakota-Montana District

Before 1920 the Dakota-Montana District had been a mission field of the Minnesota Synod. In the early days mission work was conducted mainly in the German language, because the Lutheran settlers had only recently come from Germany or the German colonies of southern Russia. Frequent summer droughts, winter storms and insect pests tried the patience and stamina of these pioneers, who were spread thinly over the vast territory. Missionaries often had to travel immense distances to reach the people they wanted to serve. The whole region, though blessed with fertile soil that yielded rich harvests in good years, was quite treeless. This made it necessary for the pioneers to build their houses of sod. Many of the first Lutheran services were conducted in sod huts.

One young missionary, just out of the seminary, told how he was met at the railway station by a member of a small congregation he was to serve and how, after a drive of twenty miles, he finally arrived at what the driver said was his home. Suddenly, while the young pastor was unloading his

Northwestern Lutheran Academy, Mobridge, S.D.

few possessions, the man disappeared. Then he heard a voice that seemed to come from below: "All right, Reverend, come on down." Soon he realized that he had been standing on a low mound forming the roof of the sod house built into a slope with the door on the lower side. "So," recalled the pastor jokingly, "my first pastoral visit was in a hole in the ground." All this, of course, is changed now.

The most significant event in the history of the district was the founding of Northwestern Lutheran Academy at Mobridge, South Dakota, in 1929. For half a century this preparatory school was the educational and spiritual center of the area until it was closed and combined with Martin Luther Academy at New Ulm, Minnesota, to form Martin Luther Preparatory School at Prairie du Chien, Wisconsin, in 1979.

More Districts

From 1920 to 1954 the Wisconsin Synod was made up of eight districts. The ninth was added in 1954 when the Arizona-California Conference was incorporated as the Arizona-California District. This district consists of the states of Arizona, California, Hawaii, Nevada, New Mexico and a tiny corner of Texas. Nineteen years later, in 1973, the South Atlantic District came into existence. All the states of Alabama, Florida, Georgia, Mississippi, South Carolina, Tennessee, part of Louisiana, North Carolina and Antigua in the West Indies are parts of this district.

At its 1983 convention the Wisconsin Synod added two more districts. One took on the name North Atlantic District and the other the South Central District. The North Atlantic District is located in the northeastern part of our country, from North Carolina on the south to Maine on the north. Several congregations of this district are in the provinces of Ontario and Quebec, Canada. The South Central District is truly in the south-central part of the United States. This district consists of all of Arkansas, most of Louisiana and almost all of Texas.

Today our church has congregations in all fifty states and in three Canadian provinces. Congregations affiliated with our synod are found on all habitable continents. In contrast to the world population, the Wisconsin Synod is a very small group indeed. Yet its modest size has not diminished the dedication of its members to the Lord's command to make disciples of all nations. Neither has their faith diminished in their Lord's promise: "Do not be afraid, little flock, for your Father has been pleased to give you the kingdom" (Luke 12:32).

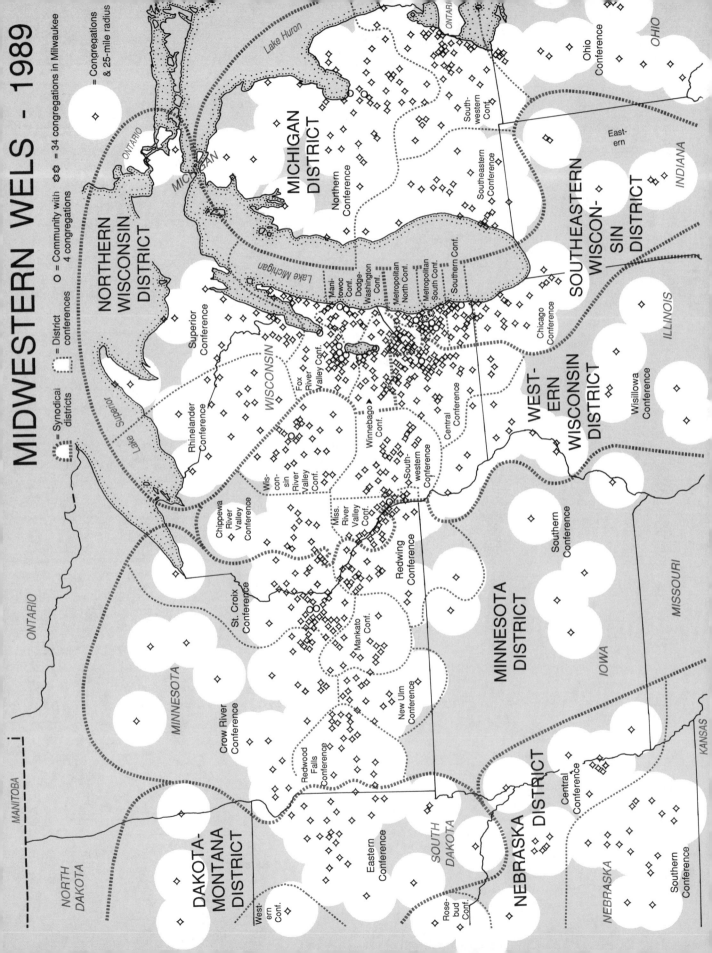

MIDWESTERN WELS - 1989

- - - - - = Synodical districts
·········· = District conferences
◇ = Community with 4 congregations
O = Community with 4 congregations
✿✿✿ = 34 congregations in Milwaukee
○ = Congregations & 25-mile radius

NORTHERN WISCONSIN DISTRICT

Superior Conference

Rhinelander Conference

Chippewa River Valley Conference

St. Croix Conference

Fox River Valley Conf.

Winnebago Conf.

Wis-con-sin River Valley Conf.

South-western Conference

Miss. River Valley Conf.

Redwing Conference

Mankato Conf.

New Ulm Conference

Crow River Conference

Redwood Falls Conference

MICHIGAN DISTRICT

Northern Conference

Southeastern Conference

Manitowoc Conf.

Dodge-Washington Conf.

Metropolitan North Conf.

Metropolitan South Conf.

Southern Conf.

Chicago Conference

South-western Conf.

Eastern Conf.

SOUTHEASTERN WISCONSIN DISTRICT

WESTERN WISCONSIN DISTRICT

Central Conference

Wisillowa Conference

MINNESOTA DISTRICT

Southern Conference

DAKOTA-MONTANA DISTRICT

Western Conf.

Eastern Conference

Rosebud Conf.

NEBRASKA DISTRICT

Central Conference

Southern Conference

Lake Huron

Lake Michigan

Lake Superior

MICHIGAN

WISCONSIN

MINNESOTA

NORTH DAKOTA

SOUTH DAKOTA

IOWA

MISSOURI

KANSAS

NEBRASKA

ILLINOIS

INDIANA

OHIO

Ohio Conference

MANITOBA

ONTARIO

Ohio Conference

Chapter 11

CONTROVERSIES IN THE SYNODICAL CONFERENCE

Plan To Form State Synods

Soon after the Synodical Conference was established in 1872, a difference of opinion over the question of forming state synods threatened to disturb the friendly relations between the Missouri and Wisconsin Synods. Actually the disagreement in this instance led to schisms within congregations and synods, thereby giving the church a bad name. Dr. C.F.W. Walther believed that there might be less friction if all the synods in each state disbanded and their congregations then united to form a single state synod. Wisconsin, fearing that it would disappear in the merger and rather doubtful of its success, opposed the plan. The leaders of our synod were not inclined to give up their identity, but rather to preserve it. For that reason they decided to reopen their own seminary in Milwaukee in 1878. Pastor Adolf Hoenecke was again called to teach dogmatics. For the next three decades until his death in 1908, Professor Hoenecke was the spiritual leader of the synod. In 1903, on the occasion of his twenty-fifth anniversary and also that of the seminary, Northwestern College and Con-

cordia Seminary each conferred the degree of Doctor of Divinity on him. The state-synod movement was soon forgotten when a larger controversy between the Missouri and Ohio Synods over the doctrine of election loomed on the horizon. In this bitterly fought battle, which began in the late 1870s and raged for ten years, Wisconsin sided with Missouri.

Election Controversy

The doctrine of election has engaged Christian theologians ever since St. Paul expounded it in chapters 8 and 9 of his letter to the Romans as well as elsewhere in his epistles. The authors of the Formula of Concord treated it at length in Article XI of that Lutheran Confession. Because it touches on the very nature of salvation, it is a comforting doctrine; and because it deals with the mystery of the unfathomable will of God, this doctrine makes no sense to human reason.

In the controversy which arose over election in the Synodical Conference, the main points discussed were these: Does God elect us to salvation wholly and entirely because of his grace and mercy? Or does he elect us because of something good in us or because he foresaw that we would one day have faith in Christ? Dr. Walther and the theologians of the Missouri Synod answered the first question with a ringing affirmative and the second with a clear and certain No.

John Calvin, next to Martin Luther the most influential of the Reformers, also answered the first question in the affirmative, but he went a step further by reasoning that, since God predestined some to salvation, it necessarily follows that he predestined others to damnation. This harsh principle of "double predestination" has always been rejected by Lutherans as unscriptural. But the men of the Ohio Synod accused Dr. Walther and the Missouri Synod of teaching the Calvinist error when he spoke of election as a choice which "God made at the pleasure of his divine will without any reference to the conduct of man."

Those who combat double predestination have often fallen into the opposite error, that God chooses his elect because of their good works. The Ohio theologians never taught such work righteousness, but they did say that God elected some people "in view of faith," meaning that God chose them because he foresaw that they would one day believe in Christ. This was obviously an attempt to give a reasonable explanation to the question, "Why, if God loves all people, did he choose only some to be saved and not others?" The Scriptures neither ask that question, nor do they answer it. It is in vain for human beings to try to explain what God has not revealed in his Word.

The Wisconsin Synod did not take part in the dispute for some years, but Adolf Hoenecke and his associates, after studying the whole problem carefully in the light of Scripture and the Lutheran Confessions, were convinced that Dr. Walther's position was scripturally correct. They then joined the Missouri theologians in declaring that we were chosen by God and so come to faith and salvation, not because of any merit in us, but because God is merciful to us sinners. He has revealed this truth of our election to assure us of the certainty of his love, not to encourage fruitless speculation as to why some are saved and others are not. If some are lost, it is because they have resisted God's grace, not because God wanted it that way. For he said, "I take no pleasure in the death of the wicked, but rather that they turn from their ways and live" (Ezekiel 33:11).

Adolf Hoenecke

The election controversy was not only a theologian's quarrel. The editor of the *Gemeinde-Blatt* published a series of articles for its readers, and several congregations studied the doctrine on the basis of Scripture and Article XI of the Formula of Concord. Not all the parishioners or pastors saw eye-to-eye in this matter. It caused a split in three congregations of our church, and four pastors left the synod. The Synodical Conference was shaken to its foundations. The Ohio and Norwegian Synods withdrew from the Synodical Conference; Missouri, Wisconsin, Minnesota and a small Norwegian group remained.

In the late 1870s the Synodical Conference had begun mission work among the blacks in the southern states. This now proved to be a bond of union among the synods of the Synodical Conference as they addressed themselves with new vigor to that work. In the middle 1930s the mission was extended into the west African country of Nigeria. Two more synods joined the Synodical Conference—the Slovak in 1908 and the Norwegian Evangelical Lutheran in 1920. The Synodical Conference became the second largest Lutheran body in America, a seemingly impregnable stronghold of conservative Lutheranism.

Postscript

During the early decades of this century several attempts were made to remove the doctrinal differences that still separated the Synodical Conference and the Ohio Synod. The latter in 1930 joined with the Iowa and Buffalo Synods to form the American Lutheran Church (ALC). Discussions between this church and Missouri—soon to be renamed the Lutheran Church-Missouri Synod (LC-MS)—continued. In 1938 Missouri adopted a resolution making it seem that ALC and LC-MS had reached agreement in all essential doctrines. Our Wisconsin Synod believed that the resolution greatly overstated the true situation and so informed its sister synod (Missouri).

About this time the Lutheran Church-Missouri Synod joined in the military chaplaincy and permitted scouting, as well as joint prayer with Lutherans with whom it was not in complete doctrinal agreement. Our church contended that these measures were unionistic and that they weakened the biblical principles of fellowship. Almost every synod convention during the 1940s and 1950s considered these issues. The synods were drifting apart, but Wisconsin hesitated to sever the tie which bound them together in fellowship for almost a century. A small group within our synod insisted on an immediate break, and when that was not forthcoming, it decided to separate and formed the Church of the Lutheran Confession.

Finally, in 1961, our church, on the basis of Romans 16:17, voted to suspend fellowship with the Lutheran Church-Missouri Synod on charges of laxity in doctrine and practice and improper relations with non-confessional Lutheran church bodies. Two years later our synod formally withdrew from the Synodical Conference.

That body became inactive in 1966 and was dissolved the following year. Our church remained in fellowship with the Evangelical Lutheran Synod (Norwegian) because it agreed with us in all teachings of God's Word.

Ever ready to confess our Savior before all men, leaders in our church prepared a twenty-four-page pamphlet titled *This We Believe*, which briefly summarizes all that we teach as a confessional Lutheran church. It points out many teachings that we must reject, but it also states that our synod is always ready to extend the hand of fellowship to all churches who hold fast to the Holy Scriptures and the Lutheran Confessions.

Unit Four
A CENTURY OF PROGRESS

59

Chapter 12

INNER GROWTH

"Wauwatosa Gospel"

In the preceding chapter the history of our church has been told up to the early years of the present century. The emphasis was mainly on its geographical expansion or, to paraphrase Isaiah 54:2, on enlarging the size of its tent.

During this time there was a corresponding inner growth, which manifested itself in various ways—in the introduction of the grade system in parish schools, in the better training of teachers, in a greater awareness of our Lutheran heritage, in increasing monetary contributions from the membership, in the opening of our first "foreign" mission among the Apaches of Arizona, and most importantly perhaps, in a distinctive, new approach to the study of the Scriptures at the seminary in Wauwatosa. This so-called "Wauwatosa Gospel" was originated and taught to the future pastors of the synod by professors Adolf Hoenecke and his successor, John Schaller, in the field of dogmatics; by J. P. Koehler in church history; and by both Koehler and August Pieper in biblical interpretation.

Briefly, these men looked upon the Bible not primarily as a collection of proof texts for particular doctrines, but in all its parts as a great preachment of the gospel of salvation in Jesus Christ. The "Wauwatosa Gospel" has lived beyond the careers of its authors, and the German works in which it was first presented are being translated and published.

Longevity in Service

There was probably less mobility among Wisconsin Synod clergymen

Prof. John Schaller

John Philipp Koehler

Prof. August Pieper

Prof. Adolf Hoenecke

in times past than there is today. More often a pastor stayed in one congregation, and the congregation was sometimes popularly called after him instead of its official name—Bendler's church instead of St. Matthew or Knuth's church instead of Bethesda. Both St. Matthew and Bethesda were once large Lutheran congregations which had been located in what is now the inner city of Milwaukee.

Professors and synod officials also served in their positions for many years. Each of the aforementioned professors served at Wisconsin Lutheran Seminary for decades. Northwestern College, in the first 110 years of its history, had three long-term presidents: August F. Ernst, Erwin E. Kowalke and Carleton Toppe. John Bading was a member of the college's Board of Control for forty-seven years, and Dr. J. H. Ott taught English at Northwestern for fifty-five years. That record was exceeded by G. T. Burk, who was a professor of music at Dr. Martin Luther College for fifty-nine years. Many other professors, including Director Otto Hoenecke of Michigan Lutheran Seminary, approached or passed the half century mark in years of teaching.

As for synod officials, in the more than a century and a quarter span between 1850 and 1989 only nine men

Prof. G. T. Burk

served the Wisconsin Synod as president: John Muehlhaeuser, John Bading (who served two separate terms), Gottlieb Reim, William Streissguth, Philip von Rohr, Gustav Bergemann, John Brenner, Oscar Naumann and Carl Mischke.

Executive secretaries (now known as administrators), treasurers and even salaried employees also tended to remain in their positions for long periods. Julius Luening was manager of Northwestern Publishing House from 1898 to 1945. During those forty-seven years most pastors identified the publishing house with him.

Chapter 13

SYNOD AND ITS PRESIDENTS

Three Presidents of the "Wisconsin Synod"

Three of the first six men to hold the presidential office were able and dedicated leaders. Though they differed greatly from one another in personality, each one in his own way set the tone for the synod and, in a sense, determined the course of its endeavors. Muehlhaeuser's simple piety and Bading's more aggressive confessional stance have already been noted. Professor Armin W. Schuetze of Wisconsin Lutheran Seminary, in his biography of Muehlhaeuser, neatly summed up what we owe to each of these two men: "Except for Bading and his sound confessionalism the Wisconsin Synod today might be part of a confessionless, ecumenical Lutheranism. Except for Muehlhaeuser, and this includes his mild confessionalism, there might never have been a Wisconsin Synod at all."

Our sixth president, Philip Andreas von Rohr, a tall, bearded, physically impressive man, was the first to be born and educated in this country. He came to us from the Buffalo Synod by colloquy in 1877 and at once assumed an influential role. Professor J. P. Koehler, who did not rate executive ability among the greatest gifts of the

Spirit, admired him as an inspired preacher and also as "a man of the world" and praised his "hospitality, open-mindedness and personal charm." Not only the members of his large congregation in Winona, Minnesota, but the people of that city pointed him out as one of the finest of their citizens.

President von Rohr
1889-1908

Von Rohr succeeded Bading to the presidency in 1889 at the time the synod was girding itself for a campaign against the Bennett law, which among other things required the teaching of the three Rs in the English language, even in German parochial schools. The law was repealed, but in the long run it had a valuable effect on education in the synod. President von Rohr came out in favor of introducing English in all synod schools, from the grades to the seminary. He spoke English fluently, even though he had not spoken the language before he was twelve. At the celebration of the twenty-fifth anniversary of Northwestern College in 1890 and again at the dedication of the new seminary in 1893, he delivered festival orations in English—one of the few pastors in the synod able to do so at the time.

During his term of office Northwestern Publishing House was established in 1891, and the federation of synods became a reality in 1892. A year later the Apache mission had its start. Though not an alumnus, von Rohr was partial to Northwestern College. With his encouragement the burnt-out "Coffee Mill" was quickly replaced in 1895, and a new dormitory was built ten years later. He then volunteered to interest alumni in a new gymnasium. Milwaukee alumni responded, but von Rohr died of cancer in 1908 before building plans got under way. "If ever the Wisconsin Synod engaged in the cult of personality," wrote seminary Professor Richard D. Balge in a biography of von Rohr, "it may have been in connection with this man.... About 2,000 people stood in the street outside the packed church (where 1,500 were in attendance) during the funeral service on a cold, clear December day in Winona."

John Bading outlived von Rohr, the man who had succeeded him after his second presidency, by five years, passing away in 1913 at the age of eighty-eight. Bading held the office of president for twenty-six years, a record later equaled by Oscar Naumann. Bading was also president of the Synodical Conference for thirty years, from 1882 to 1912. Large framed portraits of our second and sixth presidents, painted years ago by the talented Lutheran pastor and artist, L. C. H. Brockmann, adorn the north wall of the library reading room at Northwestern College. Inscribed on a brass plate attached to the gilded frame of von Rohr's painting is a tribute composed by Rev. August Bendler. Translated from the German, it reads:

> To a German oak
> Of German stock and breed,
> In the realm of heaven
> A nobleman indeed.

G. E. Bergemann
First President of
the Joint Synod

Popularly we have always been known as the Wisconsin Synod. The name is justified, since the majority of our church's membership has always been found in the three districts of Wisconsin. It is therefore quite correct to speak of G. E. Bergemann and his successors as Wisconsin Synod presidents. Actually they were heads of the Joint Synod, formed in 1917 and later called the Wisconsin Evangelical Lutheran Synod, or WELS.

President Bergemann
1917-1933

Gustav E. Bergemann functioned in two capacities. As von Rohr's successor in 1909, he was still head of the state Synod of Wisconsin. That body met for the last time in Milwaukee in July 1917. After celebrating the 400th anniversary of the Reformation in two mass services at the Milwaukee Auditorium and finishing all its business, it voted itself out of existence. President Bergemann then spoke a few heartfelt words of farewell, and the assembly rose and sang all four stanzas of Luther's hymn, "A Mighty Fortress." The secretary added a last line to the minutes: "Whether old synod or new synod, Lord, preserve Thy Word among us." The next month Pastor Bergemann was named president of the Joint Synod and reelected every biennium until 1933. His term of office, lasting nearly twenty-five years, was one of the most eventful in our church's history. It covered the years of World War I and the first —and worst—years of the Great Depression.

When Bergemann began his presidency, we were still a German church. Virtually all church services and confirmation classes were conducted in German. When his term ended, the transition to English was almost complete. Under the impact of the war and the hysteria against all things German which accompanied it, the change in languages had been accelerated, though not without soul searching and heartbreak. Many feared that our Lutheran heritage would be lost if we so hastily surrendered Luther's language and Luther's German Bible. By God's grace the opposite happened. Missionary work and spiritual growth among the young increased after we began to proclaim the gospel in the English language.

The Northwestern College gymnasium, mentioned in the previous chapter, was built in 1912 through the efforts of a group of Milwaukee alumni, who collected the necessary money and presented the finished structure to the synod. World War I intervened, and fifteen years passed before the synod was ready to undertake two major building programs—Wisconsin Lutheran Seminary on a beautiful property in Mequon, Wisconsin, and an administration building, now the academic center, at Dr. Martin Luther College in New Ulm, Minnesota. These projects strained the financial resources of the synod, especially since

Northwestern Lutheran Academy was established at Mobridge, South Dakota, about the same time, in the late 1920s.

As far back as 1905 Dr. Ott, the Northwestern College librarian, had announced that "a separate building for the library with a commodious reading room is urgently needed." Finally in 1929 blueprints for a library were ready, and the Board of Control was about to begin construction, when the depression struck. Northwestern had to wait twenty more years for its library.

Our church then entered the 1930s with a huge debt which was growing year by year as the depression deepened. Mission work had to be curtailed, and salaries were slashed. Candidates graduating from Wisconsin Lutheran Seminary and Dr. Martin Luther College found themselves without calls. Worse still, a sharp difference of opinion between the Board of Control and the faculty of Northwestern College regarding a disciplinary measure blazed into a controversy. This controversy also involved the Western and Northern Wisconsin Districts, their officials, and a group who eventually formed a separate Protes'tant Conference. Bergemann's presidency thus ended on a melancholy note, and there was no immediate prospect of relief as Pastor John Brenner assumed the office in 1933.

Brenner Presidency, 1933-1953

Gradually the synod retired its debt, and prosperity, which was brought on by World War II, returned to the country. A million dollar building fund offering, launched after the war, went over the top, and new structures began to rise at Watertown, Saginaw and New Ulm.

The highwater mark of Brenner's presidency was the celebration of the synod's 100th birthday in 1950. An anniversary of this kind in our circles is not observed by pomp and pageantry but by witnessing to the Christian faith in sermons, articles and special services—and by gathering a thankoffering. So it was during the jubilee. Its theme was expressed by the phrase "Continuing in His Word," which was also the title of a history of the synod, written for the occasion by a group of professors and pastors who had been commissioned to produce the work. The authors chose the title "as best describing the distinctive quality by

President Brenner
1933-1953

65

which the synod under God overcame the doctrinal difficulties within itself, and later those besetting it from without."

The "difficulties . . . besetting it from without" may well have referred to unhappy experiences with the Lutheran Church-Missouri Synod (LC-MS). That body had once been the champion of strict orthodoxy. It had reproved our synod in its younger years for being lax and unionistic in the doctrine and practice of fellowship. Now the roles were reversed. Wisconsin was now testifying against these same errors in Missouri, still hoping that by its testimony it might "overcome the doctrinal difficulties," so that both synods could "continue in his Word" and work together in the Synodical Conference. But the difficulties were not overcome. In 1961, therefore, Wisconsin severed the tie that had bound her to her sister synod.

Expansion and Outreach in Recent Decades

"Expansion" and "outreach" might have been the watchwords of the synod during the presidency of Pastor Oscar Naumann (1953-1979). A great, new era of building began in the early 1950s. It lasted for the next twenty-five years and eventually provided a new look for the campuses of all synod schools. At Northwestern College the only one of the old buildings still standing is the gymnasium of 1912, and it has been transformed into an auditorium. An entirely new campus, purchased in 1978, now houses Martin Luther Preparatory School in

Prairie du Chien, Wisconsin. A complex of buildings on North Avenue in Milwaukee was bought, renovated and served as the administration center of synod until 1984. In that year synod's headquarters were moved to a double building on North Mayfair Road in Wauwatosa, Wisconsin.

President Naumann
1953-1979

In 1950 our church conducted only two foreign missions—among the Apaches in Arizona and among the remnants of the Poland mission, then scattered throughout Germany in a so-called "Refugee Mission." The synod had only eight districts and one-third fewer members than it does today. The four districts which were added to the eight of 1950 are proof of the Lord's blessing on our home mission program, while the extension of foreign, now world, missions into Africa, Asia and South America has been one of the most inspiring achievements of the last twenty-five years.

President Mischke
1979-

In 1979, on the death of President Naumann, Pastor Carl Mischke, first vice president of the synod at that time and for fifteen years president of the Western Wisconsin District, advanced—and later was elected—to the presidency. In his presidential address to the Western Wisconsin District in 1966, Mischke, after speaking enthusiastically in favor of preaching the kingdom of God by extending our missions to other cities, other states and other countries, added, "It is quite possible that you and I are being permitted to live and work in what may well be the golden age of our synodical history." Only God knows whether our troubled times are a golden age for our synod. Yet the possibility is there.

Chapter 14

THE PRESIDENT OF SYNOD

The president is the chief officer of synod. His term of office runs for two years. Although subject to election every biennium, the presidents in our history, as already noted, have had a long tenure. Since 1959 the office has been fulltime. Before that the president was also the pastor of a congregation.

Our president is not like the president of a corporation, who must administer complex business operations. Most of the routine work of the synod has long since been delegated to special boards, commissions, committees and ministries, which function efficiently according to rules prescribed by the synod. Yet the president is always consulted before any major decision is made.

He is the official representative of our church and its spokesman. Whenever his busy schedule permits, he attends meetings of the synod's boards, commissions and standing committees, for he is an advisory member of each. Periodically he meets with the presidents of the twelve districts and his two vice presidents in the Conference of Presidents.

He organizes the biennial conventions of the synod, with the assistance of the vice presidents, and appoints the twenty or more convention committees which make their reports and recommendations at the meeting. He presides at the sessions and must see to it that the convention completes its business within five days. After each convention the president supervises the execution of resolutions that have been adopted. He is also responsible for making appointments to some standing committees and, in many cases, of filling vacancies in committees that occur between elections.

He is in great demand as a speaker for special services and occasions in congregations and schools and at conferences and conventions. Our president is above all concerned with the spiritual health of our church. He is a religious leader, sensitive to theological issues, serving as a "pastor to the synod's pastors," of whom there are more than 1,300.

Unit Five
WISCONSIN EVANGELICAL LUTHERAN SYNOD

CHAPTERS

69

Chapter 15

SYNOD AND ITS DISTRICTS

Synod Itself—*Statistical Reports*

Every year since 1974 synod has published a *Statistical Report* containing a variety of interesting facts about its work during the previous year. On the first two pages you can find the "Synod Totals" of its districts, conferences, congregations, Lutheran elementary schools, Sunday schools, pastors, teachers and members, together with the amounts of the contributions for home purposes, synod and charities.

In 1980 the *Statistical Report* had the synod with 10 districts divided into 45 conferences with 1,146 congregations served by 983 pastors. Communicant members numbered 309,343, and, with nearly 99,000 children the total baptized membership was 407,987. There were 30,590 pupils in 366 Lutheran elementary schools, and they were taught by 913 women and 579 men teachers. The numbers of pastors and teachers are only those who served in parishes, not those in world missions, those full-time officials, those in church-related agencies, those instructors in synod schools or Lutheran high schools, or those retired.

Sunday school enrollment was 39,943. Here the proportion of men to women teachers was even smaller:

1,211 to 4,972. Of the 99,000 baptized children probably two-thirds were of school age. That would mean that fewer than half attended Lutheran elementary schools and only a few over half, Sunday schools. Yet some 40,000 did attend vacation Bible and part-time weekly schools, and all the children received confirmation instructions before becoming communicants. In 1980, 6,422 children and 3,510 adults were confirmed.

According to the 1988 *Statistical Report*, the synod had 12 districts divided into 47 conferences with 1200 congregations served by 1140 pastors. Communicant membership numbered 317,740, but 102,000 unconfirmed children brought the total baptized membership up to 419,750. There were 31,501 pupils in 370 Lutheran elementary schools, and they were taught by 1051 women and 659 men teachers.

Sunday school enrollment was 43,414; the total number of teachers was 6535. Approximately 42,600 children attended vacation Bible school and 5316 children and 3496 adults were confirmed.

It is heartening that there has been a steady though slow growth—about one-half of one per cent per year—during the last two decades.

Organized in Districts

Each of the twelve districts, which together form the Wisconsin Synod, has well-defined boundaries. Some of the districts, like the Pacific Northwest, which includes Alaska, and the almost as large South Central, cover huge land areas but have few members.

Each district has its own officers, boards, commissions and committees. Regular district conventions are held every two years in the even-numbered years. All pastors and male teachers are expected to attend these conventions, together with a lay delegate from each member congregation.

Visit to a District Convention

District conventions are held in the summer and usually last two or three days. They are all conducted more or less in the same way. In most districts it is possible to hold the convention in a synod school or Lutheran high school, where an auditorium and plenty of rooms for committee meetings are available. The synod schools also have dormitories. If such facilities are not available in the district, the convention meets at a large church. Where a dormitory is unavailable, delegates stay in the homes of members or more commonly in nearby motels.

Each convention begins with a communion service and ends with a closing service. Pastors appointed by the district president deliver the sermons. The first order of business is the president's report, containing a review of official actions, achievements and problems of the past biennium, and suggestions for measures to be discussed and acted on by the assembly. The report is then assigned to a committee, whose members study it point by point and later offer their comments and recommendations. No matter how pressing the business of the convention happens to be, time is always reserved for one or two essays which examine religious topics of current interest in the light of God's Word. The services, devotions and essays remind delegates that the entire work of the convention is God's work and is to be carried out according to his will.

Over 400 delegates will be present at conventions in any of the three larger districts. Of these 400 about 150 will be laymen, the rest pastors and teachers.

Convention Committees

Most of the work of a district convention is devoted to reviewing the programs of the synod. Some forty boards, commissions and committees which are responsible for these synod programs submit to the districts printed reports in a book of over 160 pages. Floor committees are appointed from among the delegates to study each major report carefully. Usually a member or two of a synod board, commission or committee is on hand to supply extra information to the district committee, which then makes its recommendation to the convention. The latter may adopt, reject or amend the committee reports.

A typical district convention will have floor committee reports on the following matters of business: elections, the district president's report, home missions, world missions, evangelism, synod schools, relations with other church bodies, stewardship, membership, benevolences and pensions, parish schools and part-time Christian education, and finances.

Districts Advise

Since a district is only one of twelve in synod, it cannot adopt resolutions or vote expenditures that will be binding on all the other districts or on the synod itself. It can, however, recommend or express its disapproval of certain measures or expenditures proposed by a synod board, commission or committee. The synod at its next convention (at which all twelve districts are represented) will consider the recommendations or objections. If they are adopted, they then become binding on all the other districts, but not before.

While the district conventions are mainly advisory, they fulfill an important function. They elect the district officers and the members of the district mission board; this board supervises the mission congregations in the district. They nominate candidates for the synod's Board of Trustees and many important offices (election takes place at the synod convention in the following year). Above all, since every congregation is represented at district conventions, their reactions to existing or proposed programs are carefully studied by synod leaders as expressions of the "grass roots."

Districts Watch over Doctrine and Practice

In addition to the important functions of district conventions as mentioned above, the district also has the important duty to see to it that false teaching and harmful practices do not creep into its congregations and become established, to the spiritual harm of its members. According to the synod's constitution each district has the solemn duty to guard the purity and unity of doctrine and practice within its boundaries.

For example, if a charge is brought against a pastor, teacher or layperson who embraces and spreads false doctrine or leads an unchristian life, and if the matter cannot be settled within the congregation where the charge arose, then the matter must be taken up in the district to which the congregation belongs. That district has the duty to investigate and to settle the matter. It cannot avoid an unpleasant duty of this kind by turning the affair over to the synod. The synod acts only as a court of appeals. If the person or congregation feels that the district has decided wrongly, an appeal may be made to the synod, but only after the district has acted, and not before.

Chapter 16

CONFERENCES, CIRCUITS AND CIRCUIT PASTORS

Size and Number of Conferences

Each of the twelve districts of our church is divided into groups of congregations called conferences, and

North Atlantic District Teachers' Conference

these again are subdivided into smaller units called circuits. The number of congregations in a conference depends on how many happen to be located fairly close together. Many years ago conferences followed railroad lines, so that pastors could conveniently get to the meetings. These original boundaries are still maintained in most cases. Today the convenience of highway transportation rather than railroads determines the boundaries when a new conference is formed.

Conference sizes vary considerably. The Southeastern Wisconsin District's Metropolitan North Conference, extending over the north side of Milwaukee and into its northern suburbs, includes thirty-nine congregations and is no more than twenty-five miles from one end to the other. By contrast, the former Texas Conference, with seventeen congregations, covered the whole of that large state. In 1988 the smallest conference in number of congregations was the Apache Conference in Arizona. It had only eleven congregations served by seven pastors. In that same year the largest conference was the Central Conference of the Western Wisconsin District with fifty-five congregations which were served by sixty-three pastors.

In 1988 there were forty-seven conferences in the synod. The South Central District had only one. The conference covered the same territory and included the same congregations as the district itself. The Pacific Northwest and the North Atlantic District each had two conferences. Both the South Atlantic District and the Dakota-Montana District had three conferences. The other districts had from four to seven.

Various Kinds of Conference Meetings

Conferences meet two, three or four times a year—some for two days and some for only one—and are of various kinds. A **pastoral conference**, attended only by pastors, opens with a regular service and Holy Communion. Pastors take turns preaching the sermons. The meeting then continues with Scripture study and discussions of practical questions which confront pastors and their congregations. There is also a report on contributions the congregations are making for the synod's work. The date of each meeting, together with the program, is usually announced beforehand in *The Northwestern Lutheran*.

A **delegate conference** includes a lay representative from each congregation in addition to pastors and men teachers. The main order of its business is a thorough discussion of the program of the next synod convention. After the convention there will be another meeting of the same delegate conference to hear a report on what was done at the synod convention. Delegates then take this information back to their home congregations. In this way members are kept informed and given a chance to express their opinions about the synod's work.

Teachers' conferences devote themselves mainly to problems of what to teach and how to teach in Lutheran elementary schools. Most of the districts have a two- or three-day teachers' conference in the fall of the year. Both dates and programs are announced in *The Northestern Lu-*theran. The program usually calls for essays on a religious subject and on a timely topic related to education. There are also departmental or sectional meetings where classroom techniques and problems are considered.

Pastor-teacher conferences direct their attention to Christian education as the concern of both the pastoral and teaching ministries. Such joint meetings provide opportunities for the study of practical questions which arise in church and school, for keeping alive the spirit of fellowship pastors and teachers enjoy with one another as members of one church and for mutual encouragement. They are likely to return home from such meetings filled with fresh energy and renewed zeal to do the Lord's work.

Circuit Pastors

Each conference has a chairman who conducts the meetings, and a secretary who keeps the minutes and sends the necessary announcements to *The Northwestern Lutheran*. But the most important officers in the conference are the circuit pastors, whose duty it is to visit periodically the ten to fifteen parishes in their circuits. A circuit pastor must be a man of tact and mature judgment. He may have to encourage both a pastor and his congregation to increase their support of missions. Sometimes he is called upon for guidance and counsel when there is a dispute within the congregation or between one congregation and another. He may even have to substitute for the district president or the vice presidents when they are unable to attend a meeting at which a congregation calls a pastor.

The first sentence in Luther's *Preface to the Catechism* mentions a "visitation of the churches" which Luther himself made. On that visit he discovered such sad conditions, so many unfit pastors and teachers, and so much ignorance among the people, that when he returned to Wittenberg, he at once set about composing his *Small Catechism* in order to correct the evils he had discovered. What Luther did may serve as an inspiration to our circuit pastors today. It is the duty of the district president to watch over doctrine and practice within the district, and the president makes good use of the circuit pastors in carrying out this duty.

Chapter 17

SYNOD CONVENTIONS

The Convention "Decides"

According to our synod's constitution, which all the 1200 congregations in synod have subscribed to, all synodical property is held in the name of the synod. That includes the land and buildings of all synod schools (these do not include the area Lutheran high schools) and all mission property not owned by the local congregations. If money is to be collected for buildings, or very large amounts borrowed for any purpose, this can be decided only by the whole synod. If major property in any of the districts is to be bought or sold, the decision again rests with the synod.

The President presiding at a Synod Convention

The synod meets in convention every two years—in the odd-numbered years. The order of business is much like that of the district conventions. But there is one important difference. The delegates to the synod convention not only **advise** what is to be done, they **vote** to do it, or not. A district might advise that the synod begin mission work in South America. If the synod considers that proposal and votes Yes on it, that means the mission work in South America will begin. When a delegate to the synod convention votes Yes or No on a question, his vote carries to the very borders of synod because it does more than **advise**, it **decides**.

Convention Delegates

We call those men who vote at the convention of synod *voting delegates*. Not every congregation is represented by a voting delegate. If every pastor, male teacher and a representative of each congregation were personally present at a convention, there would be 3,500 delegates. It would be difficult to find a hall large enough for so many people, and the cost would be astronomical. So each district is entitled to one lay delegate for every 2,500 communicants. A district may choose, as an alternative, one lay delegate for every ten congregations. For every ten pastors in the district one pastor delegate is chosen, and for every ten male teachers one teacher delegate. That adds up to nearly 350 delegates, more than one-third of whom are laymen.

The officers of the synod, the district presidents and representatives of the boards, commissions and committees are required to attend the synod conventions but do not have the right to vote. About 115 of these *advisory delegates* will be in attendance.

The delegates to a synod convention bear a great responsibility. Suppose by their votes they decide to open a mission in a promising field in Africa. Their decision starts a chain of actions and expenditures that extends far into the future. It pledges all of us to train missionaries for this new field, to build houses, chapels and schools in Africa. It pledges us to support that mission adequately and effectively for the rest of our lives, or until God himself removes the obligation.

Whenever our representative at a synod convention votes, for example, to open a new mission, he must realize that he really is speaking in our name. It is as if we ourselves voted to take this step. We are therefore duty bound to supply the mission with facilities adequate for its task, to educate missionaries for that field and to support them properly with our prayers and offerings when they reach the field.

Convention Procedures

The synod's *Bylaws* require: "Conventions shall be scheduled from Monday through Friday of the first full week in August." By resolution conventions were to be held alternately at Northwestern College and at Dr. Martin Luther College. But in 1981 the synod convention met for the first time on the fine new campus of the Martin Luther Preparatory School at Prairie du Chien, Wisconsin. This school and Michigan Lutheran Seminary in Saginaw, Michigan, since 1985 have been added to the list of locations where synod conventions are held. Residence halls, unoccupied during summer, provide rooms for the delegates, and the school's food service provides the meals. Convention committees—some twenty in number—appointed to review the synod's work program, find plenty of space for their deliberations in the vacant classrooms.

The procedure or order of business at a synod convention is similar to that of a district meeting. The United States' Constitution stipulates that the nation's president shall "give to the Congress information of the state of the Union and recommend to their consideration such measures as he shall judge necessary and expedient." Our synod's president at the opening of the first session presents his "state of the synod" address, which sets forth the issues to be considered by the assembly.

Much of the business of the delegates will be devoted to hearing and debating reports of the floor committees, some of whom have been working a day or two before the convention opens to process their materials and prepare their reports. The fifty or so boards, commissions and committees have some weeks previously published their reports of the past two years' work and their plans for the next two, four and six years in a 300-page book.

It is the various items in this *Book of Reports and Memorials*, called *BoRaM* for short, which the convention committees review, evaluate and report on. Sometimes, when an important or controversial issue is under consideration, a committee will hold an open hearing at which any delegate or member of synod may argue for or against a proposed policy.

Eventually every issue or committee proposal is brought to the floor of the convention, where it is discussed— often at length—before the final vote of approval or disapproval is taken. Every effort is made to safeguard democratic procedures, so that each delegate who wishes to speak may do so. Sometimes there are so many speakers that it is necessary to limit debate, that is, to give only so many minutes to each speaker. But otherwise there is little interference with unlimited expression of opinion. Sessions are held in the morning, afternoon and evening.

The democratic process is also carried out in elections. First of all, the delegates elect the president, two vice presidents and secretary of the synod for two-year terms. Then the members of various boards are elected: seminary and college Boards of Control, the Board of Trustees and the Board for World Missions, to name just a few. Normally the term of these offices runs for six years, with the terms of one-third of the members expiring at each convention.

There are many things, of course, that are not voted on by the delegates. When the Word of God tells us plainly what we are to do, the delegates do not submit their obedience to a Yes or No vote. But in carrying on the work of Jesus Christ there can be considerable differences of opinion as to how it can best be done. Matters not decided by Scripture can be settled in a peaceful way by the use of common sense with Christian love and understanding.

Convention days are also filled with a sharing of the Word of God. The convention opens with a service of Holy Communion and also closes with a worship service, usually held at one of the local churches. Each convention session opens with a devotion. Normally about four hours are spent in hearing and discussing one or more essays on vital spiritual issues of the day. This sharing of God's Word is a constant reminder to the delegates that they are meeting under obedience to God and are in every matter to seek his will.

After the Convention

The adoption of the budget—probably one of the more important items of business—usually comes in the final hours of the convention. After it adjourns, the delegates return to their homes all over the United States, several provinces of Canada, and in world mission fields; and the day-to-day work of our church is taken over by its elected and appointed officials. Among the latter are the men of the fiscal office, who play an important role in handling and keeping records of synod funds, monies received and disbursed. Most of the church's work will be done by those often-mentioned boards, commissions and committees.

The Wisconsin Evangelical Lutheran Synod Administration Building
2929 N. Mayfair Rd., Milwaukee, Wisconsin

Chapter 18

STRUCTURE OF OUR CHURCH

Major Parts

At its 1985 convention our church resolved to make some changes in structure to improve the way in which synod and its districts do their work. Today synod's structure consists of seven major parts. They are Board of Trustees, Coordinating Council, Division of Administration, Division of Home Missions, Division of World Missions, Division of Worker Training and Division of Parish Services.

Board of Trustees

The Board of Trustees is responsible for keeping our church financially sound. It has also been directed by synod to maintain a "balanced budget"—expenditures are not to exceed income. If offerings from congregations are not sufficient to meet the budget, the Board of Trustees can direct the boards and commissions of synod to cut back on their spending. Or if the Board of Trustees deems it advisable, it is empowered to borrow money in the synod's name.

The Board of Trustees also is responsible for supervising the Church Extension Fund, which provides low-interest loans to mission congregations for purchasing land and their first worship facilities. When money is invested in this way, the Board of Trustees must make sure that the money is invested wisely.

The Board of Trustees is the synod's representative in legal matters; in fact, in the eyes of governments, the Board of Trustees **is** our church.

Membership on the Board of Trustees consists of a chairman, nine laymen and three pastors. Three laymen and one pastor are elected at each convention for six-year terms. The chairman is elected for a four-year term.

Coordinating Council

The responsibility of the Coordinating Council complements that of the Board of Trustees. The trustees are concerned about keeping synod financially sound, and the council is concerned about keeping the work program of synod balanced. According to the synod's *Bylaws*, the purpose of the Coordinating Council is to present "to each synod convention a comprehensive, balanced program reflecting a long-range planning process, by which the synod may best achieve its objectives in keeping with its total resources."

When the budget is made up every two years for the synod convention, the plans of the boards, commissions and committees usually call for the spending of more money than will be available. Humanly speaking, it seems that the needs of kingdom work always exceed the resources available. The synod, of course, does not have unlimited resources. The Board for World Missions may ask for ten additional missionaries for fields that are "ripe for harvest." The Board for Home Missions may also ask to start twenty new missions during each of the next two years. And our synod schools may ask for several new buildings and fifteen additional faculty members. If all of these "askings" were granted, the budget would far exceed the offerings of our congregations for our church's work.

The Board of Trustees has estimated the amount of money available to synod during the next two years. Using that figure, the Coordinating Council sets up a budget within those limits. It tries to balance the various requests. Perhaps the needs at the schools are so critical that home missions must be content, for the time being, with opening only seven new missions a year and world missions must be content with five additional missionaries. In this way the schools can have their new buildings and ten (not fifteen as asked) additional faculty members. It can also happen that the needs of the mission programs are so critical that the schools can be granted little of what they request. In this way the Coordinating Council weighs and balances our church's program of proclaiming God's Word.

These are difficult judgments to make because there are few, if any, programs in kingdom work that are not worthy. The Coordinating Council of fourteen men is required to make these judgments. These fourteen are the synod's president, its two vice presidents, chairman of the Board of Trustees, chairmen of the five divisional boards and six laymen. These fourteen men (you may have arrived at a total of fifteen, but the first vice president is also chairman of the Board for Administration) are elected by the synod. The administrators of the divisional boards also attend Coordinating Council meetings, but only as advisory members; they may not vote.

Division of Administration

The head administrator of our church is the synod's president, who oversees all divisions and their work. The Division of Administration was established to assist the president in carrying out the many responsibilities assigned to his office.

Among the president's helpers are the *two vice presidents*; the *secretary*; the *Conference of Presidents*; the *Commission for Communication and Financial Support*, which develops programs for establishing lines of communication between the synod's leaders and the local congregations and for funding the synod's budget; the *Commission on Inter-Church Relations*; the *Committee on Constitutional Matters*; the *Public Relations Committee*; the *Committee on Relief*; and the *Support Committee*, whose responsibility is to give financial assistance from synodical funds to pastors, professors, teachers, and their widows and orphans who experience hardship, disability or catastrophic illness.

The Conference of Presidents

The members are the synod's president, its two vice presidents, the secretary, and the presidents of the twelve districts. The primary responsibility of the Conference of Presidents is to maintain and strengthen unity in doctrine and practice among the twelve districts of our synod. Because the stewardship of money is a scriptural teaching and therefore is part of doctrine, the Conference of Presidents supervises the funding of the synodical budget (obtaining money to pay for the programs the synod has approved in convention), and it must also approve the programs for such funding. This sixteen-man group also functions as the Synodical Assignment Committee; it assigns the first pastoral positions to Wisconsin Lutheran Seminary graduates and the first teaching positions to graduates of Dr. Martin Luther College. The Conference of Presidents also calls the editor of *The Northwestern Lutheran,* our synod's official magazine, and appoints its editorial staff.

The Commission on Inter-Church Relations

Whenever a Lutheran group or church body not in fellowship with our church expresses an interest in establishing church fellowship with us, this commission of our synod meets with representatives of that group or church body. At such meetings the Commission on Inter-Church Relations professes our doctrinal beliefs and explains, on the basis of Scripture, why we believe as we do. This commission represents our church in all doctrinal discussions with other church bodies. The purpose of the Commission on Inter-Church Relations is to "extend and conserve the true doctrine and practice of the Evangelical Lutheran Church." This ten-man commission, whose members are appointed by the Conference of Presidents, consists of five parish pastors and five professors, at least three of whom are on the Wisconsin Lutheran Seminary faculty.

The Public Relations Committee

This committee, appointed by the president and vice presidents of synod, is composed of one pastor, one teacher and one layman. The Public Relations Committee informs the general public about our church's activities and explains the reasons for such activities. This committee is also responsible for keeping our church informed about governmental laws which may cause a breakdown in the separation of church and state or may hinder the preaching of the gospel. The Public Relations Committee reminds local congregations that they are the most effective public relation agencies of our church. One man is appointed director of public relations.

The Committee on Relief

As followers of Christ we not only love the one who graciously redeemed us, we also love our fellowmen. One of the ways in which we can express our love for others is by coming to their aid when they are experiencing a disaster of some kind. It can be from famine, flood, tornado, earthquake or fire. Our church established the Committee on Relief to provide relief for victims of disasters. The synod's president and vice presidents appoint five men to serve on this committee for six-year terms.

Mission Divisions

Just about half of every dollar contributed by our congregations goes to home and world mission programs. A great responsibility therefore rests upon those whose duty is to supervise this area of our church's work and to distribute the money where it will be most effective in serving our missions and sustaining our missionaries in their work of proclaiming the gospel.

More will be said about the operation of missions in later chapters of this book. Only a brief explanation about administration of the home and world mission divisions will be given here.

Division of Home Missions

There are fourteen mission districts, and each mission district is administered by a Mission Board. The fourteen district mission boards supervise mission congregations within their mission districts, approve church sites, review and approve plans for the congregations' worship facilities, and counsel mission congregations in the many problems which small and sometimes inexperienced groups have

in getting started. Since each district is permitted to elect as many members to its Mission Board as it deems suitable, the number of members on district mission boards varies from as few as three to as many as eight.

Several times a year the chairman and one layman of each district Mission Board meet as the synod's divisional Board for Home Missions. Presently this synodical board has twenty-nine members—fourteen pastors, fourteen laymen and the chairman of the board, who is elected by the synod convention.

The Board for Home Missions calls an adminstrator and an associate administrator to carry out its policies and resolutions. These two men comprise the staff of the Board for Home Missions.

Division of World Missions

In keeping with our Savior's command to proclaim his gospel of reconciliation with God to all the world, our church carries on a mission program outside our nation's borders among cultures different from ours. This program is under the supervision of the Board for World Missions.

Presently our synod's world mission program is divided into five different fields: the Lutheran Apache Mission, the Latin American Missions, the Lutheran Church of Central Africa, the Lutheran Evangelical Christian Church in Japan and the Southeast Asian Missions. Each of these mission fields is administered by an executive committee consisting of two pastors and one layman, who are elected by the synod convention.

The fifteen members of the five executive committees meet several times each year. Whenever they meet, they function as the Board for World Missions. The sixteenth member of the Board for World Missions is a pastor who is elected by the synod convention to serve as chairman. The purpose of this board is to approve budgets, to counsel on common problems and to coordinate the entire world mission program so that uniform policies and practices are observed in all the mission fields.

The called staff which serves the Board for World Missions consists of the administrator and the world mission counselor. Both of these men must be theologically trained and have pastoral experience.

Within our synodical organization the administrator functions as the board's spokesman and representative. Among his duties is his responsibility to coordinate the overall policies and programs of the board. The administrator is also expected "to search out and bring to the attention of the synod . . . openings and opportunities for the extension of the world mission program."

The world mission counselor has been called to coordinate the educational programs of the six Bible institutes and seminaries under the board's control and to counsel in matters of world mission worker training concerns. In addition the counselor develops programs for acquainting newly-called missionaries with the work they soon will be doing. The counselor assists the administrator in setting up and coordinating such programs as the World Seminary Conference and World Mission Seminars.

Division of Worker Training

This division deals with training or educating students who hope to be called into the preaching or teaching ministries of our church. The synod has six schools for such training. Three are preparatory schools (on the high school level): Martin Luther Preparatory School, Michigan Lutheran Seminary and Northwestern Preparatory School; two colleges: Dr. Martin Luther College and Northwestern College; and Wisconsin Lutheran Seminary. Each of these schools is administered by a group of men called a board of control. At present there are five (not six) boards of control in our synod. Since Northwestern Preparatory School and Northwestern College occupy the same campus, one board of control administers both schools. But each school has a president who works with the school's board of control in administering the school.

So that worker training or professional education in the synod's schools is carried out uniformly and for the best interest of our synod's purpose, a Board for Worker Training has been established. This board is composed of a chairman, elected by the synod, the chairmen of the synodical schools' boards of control, the presidents of these schools, a Lutheran high school principal, a Lutheran elementary school prinicipal and two laymen.

The official "Statement of Purpose, Objectives and Policies" of the Board for Worker Training covers nine typewritten pages. A listing of a few of the more important items will give an idea of its wide-ranging responsibilities. The board coordinates the recruitment of students, maintains capable teaching staffs, fosters sound principles and practices of intra-student and faculty relations, and proposes the tuition, room and board rates the students pay.

The board also coordinates the curricula (courses of study—the subjects taught) and the financial needs of each school, projects future needs of our church for pastors and teachers, analyzes enrollment trends, and conducts follow-up studies of services rendered to the church by those trained in our schools. It even coordinates the choir or chorus tours of the various schools.

One of the important duties of the Board for Worker Training is to "establish and present to the synod the need for land and facilities in new locations." Some years ago the board led the movement to purchase the beautiful campus of a prep school in Prairie du Chien, Wisconsin, and to merge Northwestern Lutheran Academy of Mobridge, South Dakota, and Martin Luther Academy of New Ulm, Minnesota, into Martin Luther Preparatory School.

The board has called a full-time administrator to carry out its responsibilities and its resolutions.

Division of Parish Services

This division of our church is composed of boards and commissions which are more closely associated with congregations than are the parts of other divisions. The Division of Parish Services provides services and materials to our synod's congregations which help them in their ministries of **nurture** (the spiritual growth of their members, both young and old), **outreach** (carrying on evangelism within their neighborhoods and communities), **worship** and **service**.

The Division of Parish Services consists of the Board for Parish Education, the Special Ministries Board, the Board for Evangelism, the Stewardship Board, the Northwestern Publishing House Board of Directors, the Commission on Youth Ministry and the Commission on Worship. A chairman elected by the synod and the seven chairmen of these five boards and two commissions comprise the Board for Parish Services. This board also serves as a Media Planning Board. A brief explanation of each part of the Board for Parish Services follows.

Board for Parish Education (BPE)

The synod's constitution divides the Board for Parish Education into two departments. One deals with Lutheran elementary and secondary schools and the other with part-time and adult education.

The synod expects the Board for Parish Education to encourage congregations to establish and maintain elementary and secondary schools. The board has been directed to assist congregations and to give them advice in matters dealing with education. The BPE also encourages, advises and aids congregations in establishing and maintaining part-time educational agencies. Sunday schools, vacation Bible schools and Bible classes are some of these part-time agencies. And the Board for Parish Education is expected to plan and prepare for publication new materials needed in our congregations' educational agencies, both full-time and part-time.

The Board for Parish Education is made up of four pastors, four Lutheran elementary school teachers, one Lutheran high school teacher and four laymen. All thirteen of these men are elected by the synod in convention. There are also three advisory (non-voting) members on the board. They are the administrator for worker training, a professor from Dr. Martin Luther College and a professor from Wisconsin Lutheran Seminary. Both professors are appointed by the administration of their schools.

To carry out its assigned tasks and the policies and resolutions it enacts, the BPE calls four men to serve on its staff. These staff members are the administrator for parish education, the administrative assistant for schools, the administrative assistant for part-time education and the administrative assistant for publications.

The administrator for parish education directs the overall administration of the board and acts as its representative at synod conventions and at meetings with other educational agencies.

Among the duties of the administrative assistant for schools are the promotion of studies for the improvement of instruction, the supervision of an annual testing program in our elementary schools and the supervision of an extensive school visitation program. Together with the administrator, the administrative assistant for schools encourages, advises and aids local congregations in establishing and maintaining Lutheran elementary and secondary schools.

The administrative assistant for part-time education serves the part-time educational agencies in WELS congregations. He consults with pastors and teachers on the trends and needs in this field and provides the necessary lessons and materials.

The administrative assistant for publications keeps abreast of Lutheran elementary school publication needs and plans, writes or edits courses, texts and other educational material.

The Board for Parish Education gathers and files information on schools and teachers. Upon the direction of the district presidents this confidential information is used each year to prepare several hundred biographical summaries for congregations that request assistance in calling teachers. The board cooperates with other church agencies in conducting workshops, seminars and summer courses for principals, teachers and school visitors. School visitors are appointed by the parish education coordinators of the districts with the approval of the district presidents, but the visitors report to the administrative assistant for schools.

Special Ministries Board

This board serves the synod's congregations and agencies by providing for the special spiritual needs of those who cannot be served with the gospel through regular programs of our congregations and schools. The board consists of four pastors, four laymen, one elementary school teacher and one secondary school teacher, most of whom serve as chairmen of committees which carry out the wide variety of this board's work. The Special Ministries Board serves our church through nine committees.

The **Military Services Committee** ministers to U.S. armed forces personnel and their families in Europe through two full-time chaplains. The committee also appoints contact pastors who function as part-time chaplains to synod members in the military services in the United States, South America and Southeast Asia. Additional spiritual support is pro-

Two chaplains and their wives

vided through a mailing program. Special sermons, prayers, devotional materials and *The Northwestern Lutheran* are mailed to the military services personnel.

Through the **Student Services Committee**, our synod's Special Ministries Board serves its members who are students in colleges and universities that are not affiliated with our church. This committee deals directly with the students by referring them to the nearest Wisconsin Synod congregation and by mailing them published material for their spiritual growth. This committee also recruits students for voluntary service in the synod's travel-canvass-witness program. By means of this program students are given the privilege and the opportunity to assist mission congregations in bringing the gospel to the unchurched.

At times members of our synod congregations find it necessary to move to new and distant locations. The committee with the title **WELS Membership Conservation** was established to provide referral service for such people; they are told where the nearest Wisconsin Synod church is located. Taped church services are also mailed to members who have moved to a location that is a great distance from a Wisconsin Synod church.

The **Committee on Services to the Aging** gives its attention to the spiritual needs of the elderly. It encourages congregations to become aware of the many opportunities for services the Lord places before them in the growing number of aging believers.

An important committee of the Special Ministries Board, especially for those who serve the Lord full-time, is the **Committee on Counseling for Called Workers**. The family life of our synod's pastors and teachers is important to the preaching and teaching ministry of the church. As the time for our Savior's return to judge comes closer, the society in which Christians live will grow more wicked and corrupt. This may cause the family life of many Christians in general and of pastors and teachers in particular to experience increasing stress. Such stress can have a bad effect upon the kind of work the Lord's called servants do.

The committee provides counseling for individual pastors and teachers as well as their families. Since pastors, teachers and their family memers are sinful humans, they also need strengthening of faith and rededication to serve their Lord joyfully and contentedly. This counseling has such strengthening as its purpose so that Christ's church is benefited and the Lord is glorified.

The gospel of Christ is meant for all humans, because the Lord "wants all men to be saved and to come to a knowledge of the truth" (1 Timothy 2:4). Christ died and rose to life not only for those who can learn easily, but also for people who are mentally retarded and who have other learning problems. For them to benefit from the gospel, they must learn the great truths of Christ's gospel. It is for them that the **Special Education Services Committee** does its work. This committee assists in developing skills in those who teach the mentally retarded and others with severe learning problems. The committee also prepares materials to help congregations provide for the needs of persons who are mentally handicapped.

About 12% of Americans "live" in prisons, sanitariums, mental institutions, nursing homes and hospitals. Through its **Institutional Ministries Committee**, the Special Ministries Board focuses attention on the need for spiritual service to synod members who are living in institutions not affiliated with our church. This committee also assists groups and congregations within our church who want to develop an institutional ministry program so that lay people can carry out Christ's directions to them personally: "I was sick and you looked after me; I was in prison and you came to visit me" (Matthew 25:36).

The last two committees of the Special Ministries Board deal with people who are physically handicapped. The **Committee on Services to the Hearing Impaired** is concerned for the spiritual needs of both children and adults who experience a hearing loss. The committee conducts and sponsors workshops and seminars for those who have a hearing impairment, for their families and for those who work with the hearing impaired. It also produces educational material for the spiritual training of these special people.

Blind people and those who can see very little receive the attention of the **Mission for the Visually Handicapped**. In cooperation with the Lu-

Mission for the Visually Handicapped workshop. St. Paul, MN.

theran Women's Missionary Society, this committee produces *The Northwestern Lutheran* as well as Lutheran books and tracts in braille. The committee also produces the same, as well as additional materials, on audio cassettes for the majority of the visually handicapped.

To administer its many programs the Special Ministries Board calls a full-time administrator. This man must be a college graduate with some theological training and should possess administrative abilities. He assists all regular committees of the board and carries on research for special ministries' activities.

Board for Evangelism

The root word of evangelism is "evangel" which comes from a Greek word that means "good news" or "gospel." Evangelism is telling the gospel truths to the unchurched, for they need to hear that Jesus Christ has reconciled all sinners to God, including them. Evangelism refers to our mission of sharing the gospel with those who do not know or believe in Jesus as their Savior.

There are examples of evangelism in the Scriptures. One is found in Acts, chapter 8. There we are told of the severe persecution the Christians experienced in Jerusalem. This caused many to flee to other cities, where "those who had been scattered preached the word wherever they went" (v 4). Not only did the apostles proclaim the gospel, but the Christian lay people zealously told others about the Savior. That is evangelism.

The synod's Board for Evangelism consists of four pastors, two laymen and one teacher, elected by the synod in convention. This board promotes the idea and the spirit of evangelism among the pastors and congregations of our church. To do this the board produces tools for teaching and encouraging evangelism. Some of these tools are training manuals, video tapes, tracts, Bible studies, canvass supplies, conference presentations, seminars and workshops.

Other important evangelism helps are developed by the **Mass Media Ministry**. This is a valuable arm of the Board for Evangelism, for it does much to assist congregations in their outreach programs. The Mass Media Ministry produces such outreach materials as one-minute radio ads, television public service announcements, newspaper ads and door-hanger literature. The office of this ministry also serves as a consulting agency to congregations in their use of the media to bring the gospel message to their communities.

The Board for Evangelism calls an administrator to plan and produce evangelism programs and to carry out its policies and decisions.

Board for Stewardship

Christian stewardship is the God-pleasing management of the gifts of time, talent and treasure with which the Lord has blessed his people. He wants his people to use these gifts to his glory and honor. By the faithful and God-pleasing use of time, talent and treasure Christians express their gratitude to the Lord for having been redeemed from sin and hell through the life, death and resurrection of Jesus Christ.

Our synod's Board for Stewardship was originally established to assist Wisconsin Synod members in their stewardship life. It did this by developing, designing and distributing stewardship information, programs and suggestions. This board often served the Conference of Presidents in developing programs to raise money for the synod's budget. In time this led to the complaint that there was too much emphasis on stewardship of treasure and insufficient on stewardship of time and talent.

The actions of the synod's 1985 convention brought about changes for the board. The Commission for Communication and Financial Support now serves the Conference of Presidents in funding the synod's budget, while the Board for Stewardship is a provider of stewardship information. To that end the board provides programs of stewardship education that will equip God's people for a complete life of stewardship.

The Board for Stewardship consists of four pastors, two laymen and one teacher, all elected by the synod in convention. Each district has its own stewardship coordinator, and this man is the chairman of the district stewardship committee.

Northwestern Publishing House Board of Directors

Northwestern Publishing House (NPH) is the publishing arm of our church. A board of nine directors elected by the synod governs the affairs of the publishing house. Two parish pastors, one professor from Wisconsin Lutheran Seminary, one professor from Northwestern College, one elementary or secondary school teacher and four laymen constitute the NPH Board of Directors.

The board controls and has complete authority over the financial and business affairs of the publishing house. The board hires the president for the entire operation and calls the theologically trained editors. Through its president, the board also supervises forty-five full-time and part-time employees, who provide services for people throughout the world. The board also is responsible for the publications and products sold in the retail store at NPH.

Commission on Worship

The English word "worship" had its beginning in an Anglo-Saxon word which means "honor." Definitions for the word "honor" contain such words and expressions as glory, fame, renown, high regard and great respect given. The one we creatures are to glorify, to hold in the highest regard and to give the greatest respect is the triune Lord God of Holy Scripture. He wants us to worship him (Exodus 23:25; Matthew 4:10); in fact, he is jealous (Exodus 34:14) of the glory, fame and praise that rightly belong to him alone and can be his through our worship of him.

Our church has established the Commission on Worship to help God's people worship him in church and in their homes. This commission studies the different forms for public worship, called liturgies, and it keeps itself informed about new hymns that are being written and composed. Whenever the synod directs it, the commission prepares hymnals and liturgical books. By means of pamphlets and other written material the commission also provides the members of synod with an understanding and appreciation of the music, hymns and liturgies of the Lutheran Church.

The Commission on Worship consists of three pastors, two teachers and two laymen. These seven members are appointed by the Conference of Presidents for six-year terms.

Commission on Youth Ministry

As its name suggests, the Commission on Youth Ministry (CYM) exists for the purpose of serving the youth of our church, particularly the youth of high school age. CYM is a service agency which helps congregations, conferences and districts in our synod with the task of bringing the Word of God to the youth by assisting in the training of youth counselors. The com-

mission provides training materials, such as a handbook and video training tapes. CYM conducts workshops and seminars and publishes a newsletter for youth counselors called *Youthink.*

The Commission on Youth Ministry is also responsible for materials and activities which are designed and produced for the youth themselves. CYM publishes a newspaper for the teenagers called *Generations,* and it has produced a song book entitled *Sing Unto the Lord a New Song.* In addition to these activities CYM assists planning committees which are responsible for conducting international youth rallies.

An organized synod-wide youth ministry became a commission at the 1985 synod convention. Before 1985 this group existed as a committee, which had its beginnings in the first international youth rally organized and hosted by St. Paul Lutheran congregation of Ottawa, Ontario, Canada. At that 1974 rally a temporary committee was elected and charged with the responsibility of finding a host for another international youth rally in 1975. This temporary committee, called the committee on Youth Ministry, became a part of the Board for Parish Education in 1977. The 1985 convention of our church upgraded the Committee on Youth Ministry to a commission status. That means its members are appointed by the synod president and vice-presidents. The commission consists of three pastors, two Lutheran elementary school teachers and two laymen.

Chapter 19

SUPPORTING OUR CHURCH'S WORK

It Costs Money

To maintain our home and world missions and to educate future pastors and teachers (two of the principal functions of our synod) require a great deal of money. About seventy-five cents of every dollar contributed to the synod goes for these two purposes. As our school and mission programs expanded under the Lord's blessing, the synod's budget almost quadrupled between 1960 and 1980, though inflation accounted for much of that increase. While this pace may not be maintained in each succeeding decade, it is quite likely that each year will bring to the synod more and more opportunities to proclaim the gospel. Each opportunity has its cost, both in terms of manpower and money.

Almost all of the synod's money comes to it from offerings by its congregations. A very small amount comes from special gifts and bequests. Many congregations have duplex envelopes, that is, envelopes divided into two parts. One pocket in each envelope is used for the congregation's expenses, and the other pocket is used for the synod's expenses. Some congregations have just a single envelope, and the voters' assembly determines what percent of each dollar is to be sent to the synod.

The Quota System

The synod must have some idea about how much it will receive during the year from the congregations. It must plan its expenditures, and it must be sure that it has enough money to pay its workers and running expenses. For many years the synod was on the quota system. The total budget was divided by the number of communicants and a per communicant share was arrived at. If a congregation had 300 communicant members and the per communicant share was $10, then the congregation's fair share of the synod's budget was $3,000.

There were some weaknesses in this system. It assumed that everyone's income and expenses are about the same. This is not so. For example, the average family income per year in one state in which we are heavily represented was $3,000 more than in the northern part of another state in which we are also heavily represented. There are also differences in family circumstances. One family may have no children, while another family with the same income may have five children. That makes a difference! The quota system did not take these differences into account.

Pre-Budget Subscriptions

For some years the synod has been operating under what it believes to be a more equitable system of contributions. In the fall of each year our congregations are asked to declare what they will contribute to the synod during the next year to carry on its work. Under this **pre-budget subscription system** the synod no longer tells a congregation how much it should give. The congregation, taking into consideration its own financial strength, determines for itself how much it will send to the synod. The success of the system has justified the hopes of its planners. Our people have shown a willingness to support the synod's programs because they believe it to be the Lord's work.

The Heart of Stewardship

How we use our money, together with our time and abilities according to God's plan, is called **stewardship**. The heart of stewardship is the **heart**. Good stewardship exists, not when huge sums of money are raised, but when Christian hearts warmed by the gospel of Jesus Christ are dedicated to sharing with all people the love of their Savior. God has made the United States the most prosperous nation in the world. Through this prosperity God had made American Christians mighty instruments for carrying out his plan of "reconciling the world to himself in Christ"—a rare privilege indeed.

Chapter 20

ORGANIZATIONS AND AGENCIES AFFILIATED WITH OUR CHURCH

The Lord had the Apostle Paul write, "As we have opportunity, let us do good to all people, especially to those who belong to the family of believers" (Galatians 6:10). With these words the Lord urges us to have pity on such people as the orphans, the poor, the helpless, the ill and the mentally handicapped. It is our Lord's will that we be concerned for the physical and spiritual welfare of these and other people.

Over the years, groups within our synod have established organizations which make it possible for members of our church to carry out their Lord's will as expressed in Galatians 6:10. These organizations are not owned and operated by the Wisconsin Synod, but the groups which do own and manage them are synodical members — their organizations are affiliated with our church. The following are organizations which were established after needs were realized and efforts were made to provide help for those with certain needs.

The Lutheran Women's Missionary Society

The largest of the women's organizations affiliated with our synod is the Lutheran Women's Missionary Society (LWMS). It was organized in 1964 at St. Matthew Church in Winona, Minnesota, by representatives of over 100 congregations of our church. The goal of this organization is "to increase interest in and to support mission endeavors which are a part of or in the interest of our Wisconsin Evangelical Lutheran Synod."

As the result of a request from a former synod president, Rev. Oscar Naumann, LWMS organized a Workshop for the Visually Handicapped. One of its first major projects was the publishing of *Luther's Small Catechism* in braille (a system of raised dot patterns which the blind "read" with their fingers). The workshop produces the catechism as well as other books and periodicals in braille. The services of the workshop have expanded to include audio cassettes of various publications produced in the synod. The workshop occupies permanent quarters in St. Paul, Minnesota.

Although the Lutheran Women's Missionary Society is not a synod sponsored group, all of its mission projects are approved by either the Board for World Missions or the Board for Home Missions. In addition to producing reading materials for the visually handicapped through volunteer workers, this women's organization supports such projects as radio broadcasts, mission field surveys, language study programs and new mission equipment. LWMS also helps to furnish and maintain a furlough house (duplex) and a mission house (4 units) in Milwaukee, Wisconsin, used by world missionaries and their families who are home on furlough.

The Lutheran Home
Belle Plaine, Minnesota

About twenty-five to thirty miles southwest of Minneapolis, the community of Belle Plaine is situated close to the Minnesota River. Here is the oldest health care facility affiliated with our church. The Lutheran Home came into existence during the last decade of the nineteenth century. At that time Sophie Boessling, a member of Trinity Church in Belle Plaine, made a gift of land and of $4500 for the construction of a spiritual haven for needy children and for the elderly who were without family support. The original home, with a capacity for twenty-two residents, was dedicated in 1898 and remained the only health care facility in the Wisconsin Synod for more than fifty years.

When the Lutheran Home was first established, Trinity and nearby Lutheran churches in fellowship with Trinity owned and managed the home. For the first half century of its existence the home's primary program was providing custodial and nursing care for its elderly residents. The orphanage aspect never became a major factor in its operation.

Today an entirely new facility on twenty-five acres can care for a maximum of 128 elderly and 64 mentally retarded residents. The home also offers counseling and adoption services. The Lutheran Home is now owned and operated by an association of congregations in different parts of the United States.

St. Michael's Evangelical Lutheran Home for the Aged
Fountain City, Wisconsin.

In 1860 St. Michael Lutheran congregation was established in Fountain City, Wisconsin, located along the Mississippi River. Eighty-seven years later members of this Lutheran congregation organized and incorporated their own home for the elderly.

Originally the residence, a converted house, provided a home for nine elderly members of St. Michael congregation. Since its beginning the home has expanded each time the building indebtedness was erased; this has occurred four times. Today the home can accommodate fifty-five residents. With changing circumstances the home has agreed to serve a broader clientele. In 1968 residency was expanded to include needy aged beyond our synod's fellowship, in keeping with the scriptural injunction: "As we have opportunity, let us do good to **all** people" (Galatians 6:10).

St. Michael's Home for the Aged is owned and operated by an association and a board of directors who are members of St. Michael congregation. The pastor of the congregation is also called to serve as chairman of the board and as chaplain of the home.

Martin Luther Memorial Home, Inc.

The year 1957 marked the beginning of Martin Luther Memorial Home, Inc. It was in that year that meetings were held at Trinity Church in Saline, Michigan, to explore the possibility of establishing care facilities for elderly Christians. In May of 1958 representatives from twenty-seven Michigan congregations met in Plymouth and formed an association named Martin Luther Memorial Home, Inc.

A plan was formulated to establish a convalescent and nursing facility in each of the four Michigan District conferences. The first facility was dedicated in South Lyon, where a home was acquired that provided accommodations for eighty people. In 1971 an 84-bed nursing home was purchased in Holt and two years later a 71-bed nursing home was obtained in Saginaw. In 1981 a nursing home for 125 people was purchased in South Haven. All four homes provide skilled nursing care.

The association has grown to ninety Michigan District congregations. It operates the four homes through an elected board of directors, made up of twelve men. Each home has its own administrator, and the central office for the executive administrator is located at South Lyon.

The motto and continuing concern of the Martin Luther Memorial Home, Inc. is CHRISTIAN CARE FOR AGING CHRISTIANS.

Wisconsin Lutheran Child and Family Service

In 1965 a group of interested Wisconsin Synod pastors and laymen purchased a 113-bed nursing home on Milwaukee's northwest side and incorporated itself under the name Wisconsin Convalescent Home.

It soon became apparent that an increasing number of synod members were interested in enlarging the scope of services. So a decision was made in January 1966 to change the name of the organization to Wisconsin Lutheran Child and Family Service (WLCFS). At the same time the following goals were adopted: To care for the spiritual needs of children, unwed and adoptive parents, troubled families, the elderly, the convalescent and the handicapped. Such spiritual care would be given in a Lutheran program of custodial care, consultation, casework service and the operation of foster homes. This combination of endeavors brought overwhelming support from our church members and led to several enlargements in the physical plant.

Under the leadership of its first executive director, Rev. Ernst F. Lehninger, new programs were added in family counseling, foster care, alcoholism recovery and services for the mentally retarded. Area offices have been opened at Appleton, Eau Claire, Madison and Wausau in Wisconsin and at Morton Grove in Illinois to serve the areas with concentrations of members.

WELS LUTHERANS FOR LIFE

WELS Lutherans for Life

The purpose of WELS Lutherans for Life is to educate people in the value and sanctity of human life and in the related issues of abortion, infanticide and euthanasia. The organization develops and supports programs that protect and maintain life in conformity with the teaching of God's Word. These programs provide an avenue for reflecting Christ's love and sharing his message of salvation.

The seeds for WELS Lutherans for Life were sown in 1975. A group of Christians from a WELS congregation in Libertyville, Illinois, was troubled by the soaring number of abortions. It formed a pro-life committee and encouraged other congregations to do the same. In 1980 WELS Lutherans for Life was formally organized and a national board was elected in 1983.

The educational and gospel outreach mission of WELS Lutherans for Life is carried out by the chapters and branches of the organization. A branch is a pro-life group within a congregation and seeks primarily to educate its members in life issues. A chapter represents members from a number of area congregations within the fellowship of WELS. It carries out educational programs in life issues usually on a larger scale than do branches.

One of the major educational agencies of most chapters is sponsorship of a pregnancy counseling center. Through these agencies trained volunteers share biological facts about life in the womb as well as the spiritual message of sin and grace.

Branches are under the supervision of the pastor and congregation leaders and are considered to be part of the congregation, governed by its rules and regulations. Chapters elect their own boards of directors and are considered part of the national organization of WELS Lutherans for Life and subject to its rules and regulations.

The national organization provides assistance to branches, chapters, pastors, lay people and congregations from its office in Milwaukee, Wisconsin.

Lutheran Pioneers, Inc.

Lutheran Pioneers is a Christ-centered program for boys within the fellowship of the Wisconsin Synod. The purpose of this youth organization is to provide boys of Lutheran congregations with a program in keeping with the purpose of our church. There are various ways in which Lutheran Pioneers carries out its purpose. Among them are teaching boys God-pleasing citizenship, knowledge of God's creation and skills for survival in God's great outdoors.

There are three levels within the Pioneer program. They are the Buckaroos (for boys in first, second and third grades), the Pioneers (for boys in fourth grade and older) and the Troopers (for boys who have been confirmed). At each level specific skills are taught. Some of the skills are flag etiquette, basic and advanced knots, basic and advanced first aid, basic and advanced camping, nature study, survival and leadership skills.

The national headquarters of Lutheran Pioneers, Inc., is in Burlington, Wisconsin.

Lutheran Girl Pioneers, Inc.

The beginnings of this organization for Lutheran girls go back to 1954, when a girl's club was organized at Mt. Calvary Church in La Crosse, Wisconsin. In May of 1955 representatives of six Wisconsin Synod congregations in Wisconsin and Minnesota met to draw up a constitution for Lutheran Girl Pioneers, Inc.

A national council, composed of elected and appointed members, governs this organization. A national counselor, two assistant national counselors and a vice-national counselor carry out the policies and decisions of the national council. The United States and Canada are divided into twenty-four districts, and each district is divided into caravans. Girls from grade one through high school may become members of Lutheran Girl Pioneers. The girls are part of either the Sunbeams (for those in grades one and two) or the Pioneers (for those in grade three through high school). The Pioneers are divided into Travelers, Trailblazers, Homesteaders and Spinners.

"Loyal to Christ" is the motto of the Lutheran Girl Pioneers. To carry out this motto the organization has a three-fold purpose: (1) to grow in the knowledge of God's Word; (2) to enjoy more fully the beauty of God's creation; (3) to experience the joys of Christian fellowship.

The WELS Historical Institute

The WELS Historical Institute is our synod's official agency for the promotion of historical interests.

According to its constitution the institute has several purposes. These include (1) to promote interest in the history of Lutheranism, particularly of the Wisconsin Evangelical Lutheran Synod; (2) to stimulate historical research and to publish its results; (3) to collect and preserve articles of historical value to our synod; (4) to serve as the synod's official department of archives and history.

The institute publishes a historical journal twice each year. This journal is sent to all members of the institute. The institute also maintains the synod's museum, which is located in the Salem Lutheran Landmark Church, built in 1863 on the site of the birthplace of our synod. This church building is situated on the northwest side of Milwaukee. The synod archives, located at Wisconsin Lutheran Seminary, are another area of historical importance. The synod's archivist is a member of the institute's board of directors.

Membership in the WELS Historical Institute is open to any interested church member. The same is true of institute meetings at which historical presentations are given.

The seal or logo of the WELS Historical Institute depicts Salem Lutheran Landmark Church. The Wisconsin Synod was born in 1850, and in 1981 the WELS Historical Institute came into being. The German inscription is a reminder of our synod's German roots. The German words mean "Remember the former time." The cross reminds us of our Savior Jesus Christ, the Lord of all history.

Unit Six

CHRISTIAN EDUCATION IN OUR CHURCH

CHAPTERS

Chapter 21

TEACHERS AND SCHOOLS IN THE EARLY YEARS

Preachers Teach and Teachers Preach

In our church Christian teaching has a tradition almost as long and honored as Christian preaching. In the very first convention of the Wisconsin Synod, in May of 1850, it was resolved that every pastor should "devote himself especially to the young and conduct a day school, and Bible and mission classes." During the 1850s probably more pastors than teachers were instructing the children in our congregations. The report of the ninth convention in 1858 lists fourteen pastors, sixteen day schools, seven Sunday schools, but only three teachers.

While it was often difficult to find a trustworthy pastor, it seems to have been even harder to find a good teacher. There were men who passed themselves off as teachers, though they had no training at all and had only the haziest notion of what Lutheranism was. Sometimes they were little better than tramps, and congregations that hired them to teach their children religion and German were greatly disappointed.

Fortunately there were always a few able and faithful teachers at hand. Some of them had to substitute for the pastor and read a sermon to the congregation on those Sundays when the pastor was preaching in one of his smaller churches. In a few cases teachers even qualified as pastors. In 1858 the congregation at Jefferson, Wisconsin, after looking in vain for a preacher, called a Watertown teacher, E. Rupnow, to become its pastor. Rupnow had for some time traveled from Watertown and conducted reading services in the congregation's little log church. He accepted the call and served the congregation for five years. Though somewhat lacking in theology, he was successful in gathering members and helping them to build their second, larger church.

In that same year, 1858, Teacher Frederick Hass of Woodland, Wisconsin, was called to be the pastor of a newly organized congregation of forty families in Hustisford. His salary was $80 a year and enough feed and pasture for ten cows. He also taught forty pupils five days a week. In Lebanon, Wisconsin, Teacher Pankow, excommunicated because he played dance tunes on his fiddle, became the shepherd of an independent congregation and served it for many years.

No Bed of Roses

The lot of our first Lutheran teachers was not exactly a bed of roses.

They had no professional contacts with each other in conferences of their own, nor were they allowed to attend pastoral conferences or even to be considered members of the synod. It was not until 1872 that a number of teachers in southern Wisconsin petitioned the synod to accept them as members. The pastors were willing to grant them that privilege and also invited them to attend pastoral conferences, but without the right to vote. But before they could enjoy any of these privileges, they would have to pass a colloquy (oral examination) to prove that they were true Lutherans. Pastors in those days were a very exclusive group. The teachers protested, and it was finally agreed that if a teacher had served faithfully and instructed children in a Lutheran congregation for a number of years he would not be subjected to a colloquy to prove his faith.

In that same year, 1872, the teachers were encouraged to organize their own professional conference in Wisconsin. In 1947, when this teachers' conference celebrated its seventy-fifth birthday, it published a booklet containing excerpts from the minutes of its early meetings and a history of Wisconsin Synod parish schools. Much of the following is taken from that interesting account.

Teachers' salaries were pitifully small and their vacations brief—only four to six weeks during the summer. The parochial school year usually ran to the end of June and began again the middle of August. The public schools, in contrast, opened in Sep-

tember and closed in May. In some areas it became the custom, lasting well into the first decade of the present century, for parents to send their children to the little red public schoolhouse during the regular term to learn English, and to the parochial school for a few weeks to learn religion and German.

One of the greatest burdens of a teacher in the early years was the tremendous size of the classes. The school report of 1880 revealed that fifty-five teachers and thirty pastors were then teaching 4800 children—an average of nearly sixty per teacher. Actually there were many schools in which a single male teacher in a single classroom was teaching—or trying to teach—over 100 pupils. The all-time record was probably that of the upper class at St. Jacobi School in Milwaukee; it numbered 123—all in one room under one man. In addition, many of the men had to supplement their small salaries by giving music lessons, writing for German newspapers or working on farms. One even did a little doctoring on the side until he was reprimanded by the synod.

Language Problems

Our early Lutheran schools were often called "German schools" because all subjects were taught in German. Children learned reading, writing, arithmetic and memorized the catechism, Bible passages and hymns in German because it was the language of home and church. But America was an English-speaking country, and children who grew up speaking only German were at a disadvantage. Lutheran teachers tried to meet the growing demand for more instruction in English but were at a disadvantage themselves, since most of them did not speak English well enough to teach it to the children.

Reports of conference meetings reveal the discussions that were going on year after year concerning the language problems and how to solve them. One suggestion was that every school should hire an English teacher, not necessarily a Lutheran, to teach the three Rs. That idea was rejected as "deplorable." Others agreed that most of the teachers knew enough English to teach it by the cumbersome method of translation from the German. Others thought the problem might be solved by assigning passages from the English Bible or the English poets for memorization. Most realized that the only way would be for the teacher to learn to speak English fluently and conduct the class in English, using English textbooks. Eight English articles that appeared in issues of the teachers' *Schulzeitung* (School Magazine) in 1886 reflect the general interest in preparing for the eventual change in languages.

Wisconsin's Bennett law of 1889, with its requirement that the basics be taught in English even in German parochial schools, produced a new round of discussions concerning the language problems. Though the law was repealed in 1891, the synod appointed a committee to examine English school textbooks and to work out a uniform plan of instruction both for a one-class and a four-class school (the eight-grade system was not then in use in our schools). But progress was slow. Around 1900 arithmetic was still taught in German, and it was not until 1913 that the conference debated the question of using English as the medium of instruction in religion, and then tabled it. By that time the eight-grade system along with English textbooks had been introduced in most of the schools, and Rev. Carl Gausewitz was at work on a translation of the catechism into English. Even without the pressure brought on by World War I, the schools had developed to a point where the change from German to English meant only an increase in efficiency.

Schoolmasters vs. Schoolma'ams

The first woman teacher to make her appearance in the classroom of a synod parish school was the wife of Teacher Voss of Watertown, Wisconsin, who instructed some of the lower grades in St. Mark School during the winter months of 1875. That same year the *Schulzeitung* published a note that one female student of Northwestern academy was ready to accept a teaching position. The Winona congregation, according to a report in the *Gemeinde-Blatt* in 1880, was ready to hire a *Lehrerin* (the new name for women teachers) as assistant, if the number of pupils in their school rose above 112.

By 1892 there were twenty-two *Lehrerinnen* teaching in our Lutheran schools. They had breached the pedagogical ramparts, but the male defenders were not yet ready to concede defeat. At a conference in 1896 Teacher Wedekind read a paper titled "The Woman Teacher in Our Congregational Schools." The essayist deplored the hiring of women teachers by congregations because their salaries were lower. It was a mistake, he said, to think that young children away from their mother's care for the first time would do better under a woman teacher than under a man. The essay provoked a great deal of favorable comment. Some even wondered whether the employment of women teachers conformed with Holy Scripture, since Paul had forbidden women to speak in the church. Teacher Schwartz, in an article in the *Schulzeitung*, thought that a woman teacher might be permissible for the very young, if a qualified man was not available. But a woman ought never to be allowed to teach older children, certainly not boys. "Anyway," he wrote, "teaching is not a woman's job." Yet in the next year, 1897, Dr. Martin Luther College introduced coeducation and invited women to enroll.

Women teachers were not allowed to attend conferences until after the turn of the century. Finally in 1908 the chairman not only extended them an official welcome, but the conference, probably as a result of their presence, voted to discontinue smoking at meetings from that time on. The women had to wait until 1910 before one of them was asked to appear on a conference program. That honor went to Miss Marie Scheuer. The next two women to appear were Miss L.

Karth and Miss Johanna Brockmann. When the latter retired in 1933, she had taught for nearly fifty years in various schools affiliated with our Wisconsin Synod.

But the schoolma'ams had not yet proved their mettle in the eyes of men. In 1912 Teachers Wedekind and Klatt held forth on the topic "How Ought Women Teachers To Be Trained in Order to Qualify for Their Position," and in the following year they followed up with another essay "At What Grade Is the Appointment of a Woman Teacher Justifiable?" Even as late as 1929 the School Committee in reporting to the synod stated that the increasing proportion of women teachers constituted "a real danger to our schools and to our whole Christian life."

In 1947 there were 150 women teaching in parish schools—compared with 200 men. By that time no one would have thought of calling in question either their efficiency in the classroom or their devotion to their high calling. And so it still is today when women teachers outnumber men in our Lutheran elementary schools.

St. Andrew Lutheran School, Chicago IL.

Schulzeitung, Texts, Tests, Organs

For many years there were more teachers who did not take the colloquy for synod membership than those who did. Besides, attendance at the conference meetings was so poor that for a dozen years during the 1880s teachers met only briefly during synod meetings whenever they could find a suitable room and a free hour or two. A temporary chairman was then named, but no minutes were kept.

In 1876 an active group of teachers founded their own school paper, the *Schulzeitung*. It was edited and mainly written by Northwestern professors F. W. A. Notz, A. F. Ernst and A. L. Graebner, though teachers also contributed articles. The synod took over the publication of the magazine in 1878. Some of the material published reflected the latest German views on elementary education and is still worth reading. But the *Schulzeitung* never had enough subscriptions to cover the cost of printing, even after Prof. J. Schaller of Dr. Martin Luther College became its editor in 1893. At last in 1905 the synod terminated the magazine because "too few readers felt it worthwhile to send in the modest subscription price of one dollar." More than thirty years passed before the teachers again had their own periodical, the *Lutheran School Bulletin*, forerunner of the present *Lutheran Educator*.

A perennial problem of our Lutheran schools was to find adequate textbooks. The synod published its own catechism modeled on the one used in Dresden, Germany. German readers and *Fibels* (primers) adapted to our schools and printed here were standard texts. Prof. Ernst wrote a German Bible history, which was in use until an English translation, prepared by Prof. J. Meyer, was introduced in the 1920s. Rev. J. Brockmann of St. Mark Church in Watertown, Wisconsin, and Teacher H. Seifert each published popular collections of German songs and carols. A German *Rechenbuch* (arithmetic) by Teacher Schwartz was widely used. Prof. Graebner supplied an *English Composition and Grammar*.

Then as now congregations wanted teachers who could perform well on the organ. But when Northwestern introduced its teachers' course in the 1870s, it did not have an organ for students to practice on, until one day a crated instrument arrived at the door of the residence hall. Rev. Brockmann, having heard of an available second-hand organ, had bought it on his own. The next number of the *Schulzeitung* called for contributions to reimburse him for the $50 he had advanced. It reported that music students at Northwestern were practicing on the organ to their heart's content. Dr. Notz even quoted a humorous couplet to describe their enthusiasm:

> *Ja, mich ergreifen hoehere Gefuehle,*
> *Wenn ich mit Hand und Fuss in Toenen wuehle.*
> *(Oh, what high and noble feelings follow*
> *When with hand and foot in tones I wallow.)*

The last class—five men and two women—graduated from the five-year course in education at Northwestern in 1893. Dr. Martin Luther College then took over the training of teachers for the synod. Its course, beginning with prep school, also ran for five years, but such was the demand for teachers that many finished their studies in three or even two years. This trend was reversed when a sixth year was added to the course in 1920.

Up to the middle 1880s it was the custom to have public examinations of pupils in the parish schools. Northwestern College and the seminary also held public examinations at the end of each school year. Examination day seems to have been a rather festive occasion. In a quaint description found in an old manuscript preserved among the records of Grace Church in Milwaukee, it is called "a great event."

> Children cleaned and scrubbed everything in the school. Boys gathered cedar twigs in bags in the country; these were made into garlands. The girls made pink and white roses of tissue paper with which to decorate the schoolrooms. Children were dressed in their finest. The parents came in the afternoon to hear and see what progress their children had made.

But in 1885 the teachers persuaded the synod to discontinue the examinations in parish schools. The only reason given was that they had been "a necessary evil."

School Sermons and Sunday Schools

At the ninth synod convention in 1858 one of the pastors preached on "The Importance of Christian Education." The preaching of a "school sermon" at the annual synod convention was repeated at intervals but seems to have been discontinued, for in the 1880s the teachers requested that one sermon at each convention be dedicated to the topic of Christian education. This became an established rule, even in the biennial district conventions of later years.

In 1858 seven of our churches already had Sunday schools. They were not like the ones we know today but probably the equivalent of those "Bible and mission classes" that pastors were to teach according to a resolution passed at the first synod convention. They were usually scheduled for Sunday afternoons and conducted by pastors.

When modern Sunday schools were introduced in the churches, many people feared that they might crowd out the Lutheran elementary schools. That did not happen. The two institutions flourished side by side, and each served its own purpose. Sunday schools provided Christian education in congregations unable to support an elementary school. They were also an excellent means of doing mission work. Unchurched children were won for Christ, and through the children the Lord often led unchurched parents into his fold.

Chapter 22

PARISH SCHOOLS, HIGH SCHOOLS AND A COLLEGE

Parish Schools Today

Our modern parish schools, compared with those of a century or even half a century ago, have shown remarkable growth both in numbers and quality. During the last decade, the pupil/teacher ratio was 19.5 to one and for the kindergarten 14.1 to one. What a difference from the overcrowded classrooms of the pioneer era!

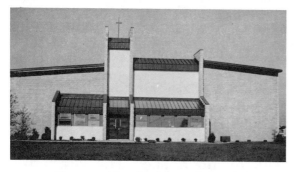

Resurrection Lutheran School,
Rochester, MN

The teaching profession in general enjoys more prestige today than it did in times past. In our church teachers are especially honored as men and women engaged in a teaching ministry, which encourages Christian children to fear their Lord (Psalm 34:11) and to serve him in all God-pleasing occupations. A college degree from Dr. Martin Luther College or an equi-

valent institution is now considered essential for teachers. Those who have graduated from secular colleges are required to take religion courses to be certified as fully qualified teachers in our Lutheran elementary and secondary schools.

Soon after World War II, congregations began to replace the old one-room schools with fine new buildings that were furnished with facilities of all kinds from teaching aids and textbooks to playgrounds and gymnasiums. And teachers' salaries were raised.

Lutheran High Schools

The first area Lutheran high school was founded in Milwaukee, Wisconsin, as long ago as 1903 by an association made up of Wisconsin Synod and Missouri Synod congregations. The school has played an important role in Lutheran culture in the city, for many of its graduates have entered the teaching profession, and others have become leaders in their respective congregations. After more than fifty years of joint work, the Milwaukee congregations of each synod built their own high school. The association of Wisconsin Synod congregations built its high school on the west side of the city and named it Wisconsin Lutheran High School.

The second area Lutheran high school affiliated with our church, Winnebago Lutheran Academy in Fond du Lac, Wisconsin, came into existence in 1925. In the 1950s five additional high schools were established. Those in the state of Wisconsin were Fox Valley Lutheran in Appleton, Manitowoc Lutheran in Manitowoc, Luther in Onalaska and Lakeside Lutheran in Lake Mills. In Minnesota it was Saint Croix Lutheran in West St. Paul. After a lull in the opening of new high schools during the next decade, the high school movement picked up momentum in the 1970s. The following chart lists the area Lutheran high schools that are affiliated with our church and the year each was founded:

Arizona Lutheran Academy

Name	Location	Date of Founding
Arizona Lutheran Academy	Phoenix, AZ	1978
California Lutheran	Garden Grove, CA	1977
East Fork Lutheran	Whiteriver, AZ	1948
Evergreen Lutheran	Kent, WA	1978
Fox Valley Lutheran	Appleton, WI	1953
Huron Valley Lutheran	Westland, MI	1975
Illinois Lutheran	Crete, IL	1986
Kettle Moraine Lutheran	Jackson, WI	1974
Lakeside Lutheran	Lake Mills, WI	1958
Luther	Onalaska, WI	1957
Manitowoc Lutheran	Manitowoc, WI	1956
Michigan Lutheran	St. Joseph, MI	1970
Minnesota Valley Lutheran	New Ulm, MN	1979
Nebraska Ev. Lutheran	Waco, NE	1979
Northland Lutheran	Wausau, WI	1979

Name	Location	Date of Founding
Saint Croix Lutheran	West St. Paul, MN	1958
Shoreland Lutheran	Somers, WI	1971
West Lutheran	Hopkins, MN	1979
Winnebago Lutheran Academy	Fond du Lac, WI	1925
Wisconsin Lutheran	Milwaukee WI	1903

The Association of Lutheran High Schools in cooperation with the synod's Board for Parish Education has developed a system of workshops, visitation

View of the WLC Campus

and self-study programs to improve instruction and help the teachers guide Lutheran youth during the difficult teen-age years following confirmation.

Wisconsin Lutheran College

It was only natural that with the success of Christian training in its secondary schools, the Wisconsin Synod should plan to extend Lutheran education to the college level. In its convention of 1959 at Saginaw, Michigan, the synod resolved to open a junior college in the Milwaukee area the following year. Rev. Robert J. Voss was called as its president. Though intended chiefly as a worker-training school to help fill the need for more teachers, many hoped that it might also become a Lutheran college for the future laity of our church. Wisconsin Lutheran College grew rapidly, reaching an enrollment of 228. Its graduates finished the last two years of their training at DMLC in New Ulm, Minnesota. But when the critical shortage of teachers was relieved, the doors of WLC were closed in 1970, and it was merged with Dr. Martin Luther College.

In 1978 a second Wisconsin Lutheran College was established in Milwaukee by a national association of our congregations, in time numbering sixty-nine. The new WLC is located in an impressive complex of buildings—a former cloister—in the suburb of Wauwatosa. It was begun as a two-year, coeducational, liberal arts college but in 1985 it became a full-fledged four-year college. Wisconsin Lutheran College prepares its students for secular professions, but with a major emphasis on lay involvement in the work of the church at large. Dr. Gary Greenfield became the first president of the second Wisconsin Lutheran College.

Confirmation Instruction

At the time of the first convention of our synod in 1850 fifty-five people were being instructed for confirmation by the little group of pastors. Of all types of Christian education offered in the Lutheran church, confirmation instructions are the most intimate and cherished. They tend to have a lasting influence on the lives of Lutheran Christians.

The rite of confirmation goes back many centuries and was brought to this country by our German forebears. It has been a time-honored institution ever since, and all adult Lutherans today have at one time or another—usually at the age of thirteen or fourteen—attended a course of instruction given by their pastors in preparation for confirmation and first communion. There is something inspiring in the thought that our church's more than one thousand pastors, old and young, each year instruct thousands of boys and girls at the threshold of adult life in the life-giving truths of the Book of Life as they are summarized in Luther's *Small Catechism*.

Chapter 23

MINISTRY OF THE PRINTED WORD

Northwestern Publishing House

Though there are no teachers, desks or preachers' pulpits at Northwestern Publishing House, it is essentially an educational institution, supplying the religious books, lessons, literature and other publications used in our churches, schools and homes. It is engaged in a teaching ministry—a ministry of the published word for all age levels and for all our people.

NPH receptionist area

The publishing house welcomes visitors and tour groups. Visitors are invited to browse in its bookstore, where many different books and gift items are on display and offered for sale. Those desiring a tour are conducted through the modern building by a guide. A leaflet handed to tour members contains a brief account of the history and varied services of NPH.

From it one learns that NPH was founded in 1891 to be the official agency of the synod for printing, publication and distribution of all such books, periodicals and literature considered beneficial to the Lutheran faith. The bookstore began fifteen years earlier in 1876 in a picture-framing shop on Broadway in Milwaukee, Wisconsin, but was merged with the printing establishment when the latter opened in rented quarters on Third Street.

After two more moves in the same neighborhood, NPH finally had a permanent home when its Board of Directors purchased land and erected a three-story building on Fourth Street in 1914. But thirty-four years later the city of Milwaukee served notice on the publishing house to vacate the premises because the area was to be the site of a new sports arena. The board then purchased and remodeled a large vacant store building on North 37th Street and West North Avenue. In

View of the store

1949 it was chosen for the honor of being the most attractively redesigned building in Milwaukee. In 1985 the publishing house experienced another move into a one-story building constructed according to the board's specifications. This new home for NPH is located in the suburb of Wauwatosa.

Up until 1985 the publishing house did its own printing and binding. But these activities were discontinued in that year.

Almost any need of the Christian church or school, from choir music and choir robes to tape cassettes and communion ware can be supplied by the publishing house. Bible histories, Bibles, catechisms, hymnals, devotional books, religious pictures and rings are some other items available through the retail store and catalog department.

Periodicals and Other Publications

Practically every church body has at least one official church paper. Our synod's is *The Northwestern Lutheran*. It has been appearing every two weeks since January 7, 1914, until recently. Now it is published semi-monthly, except monthly in July, August and December. Over the years its purpose has remained the same. It contains editorials, devotions, Bible studies and articles that lead to a better understanding of Scripture and keep readers informed on activities of our church. It also answers questions such as the following: Are we training enough workers? How many mission fields do we have and what progress is being made in them? What are some of the special problems facing our church? Is there a great need that requires more attention and more generous giving on our part? To learn the answers to these and similar questions, church members read *The Northwestern Lutheran*.

Our synod publishes a magazine intended chiefly for pastors—the *Wisconsin Lutheran Quarterly*—another for Lutheran elementary school teachers—*The Lutheran Educator*—and another for persons interested in other forms of Christian education such as Sunday school, VBS, Bible class and confirmation class—*PARTNERS in Christian Education*. Each magazine appears four times a year.

Though not a periodical, the *Yearbook*, published by NPH each year in December, is found in many homes. It contains the names and addresses of all pastors and teachers, besides a church calendar, a directory of all congregations and schools, of all synod services, and other useful information.

The publication found in more homes of our church than almost any other is *Meditations*. It is not directly sponsored by the synod but is published by Northwestern Publishing House. *Meditations* is a booklet appearing quarterly; each page consists of a Scripture reading, a meditation and a prayer, besides additional daily and special prayers.

Besides the publications mentioned, there are any number of special letters, tracts, pamphlets and periodicals issued by various boards and commissions of the synod. As far back as 1923 the Arizona missionaries began publishing a little paper, the *Apache Scout*, which the secretary of the Mission Board at that time welcomed with these words: "God speed you, little Scout. Carry the greetings of the Mission Board to every Apache Indian, old and young, and tell them that we want nothing so much as to have them get the good things which Jesus Christ obtained for us, the forgiveness of sins and life with him in heaven."

In recent years almost every board and commission began producing special literature. For example, after each synod convention an eight-page newspaper, the *Wisconsin Synod Herald*, is published to present the convention highlights. The synod president periodically sends out to all pastors and teachers the *President's Newsletter*; the Board for Parish Education produces *Notes and News* and *Principal's Newsletter*; and the Commission on Youth Ministry publishes *Generations* for the youth and *Youthink* for the group leaders. There is also a rental library of films, filmstrips, and audio and video cassettes in the audiovisual department at Northwestern Publishing House.

Unit Seven

TRAINING THE LORD'S SERVANTS IN OUR CHURCH

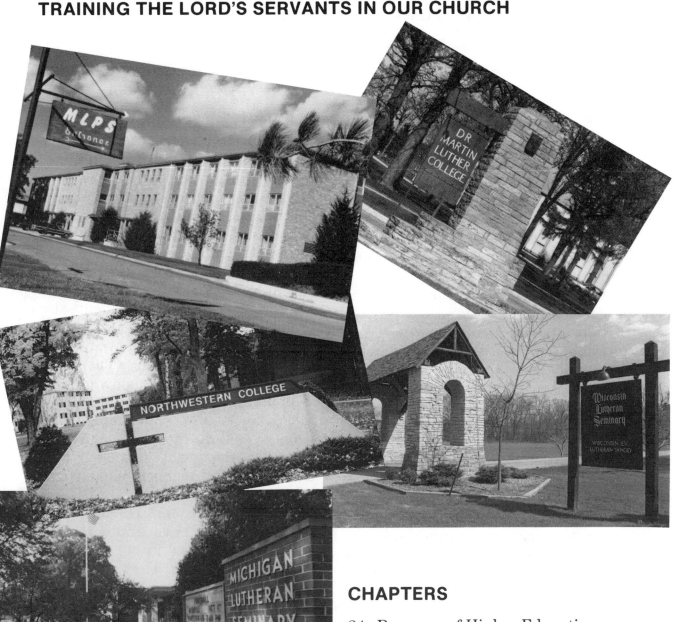

CHAPTERS

115

Chapter 24

THE PROGRAM OF HIGHER EDUCATION

How Vacancies Are Filled

According to a recent *Statistical Report*, 198 pastors and 116 teachers accepted calls or received their first calls after finishing their studies during that particular year. At any given time we can expect that there will be pastor and teacher vacancies in our church.

When a vacancy occurs in a congregation because a pastor retires, dies or accepts a call elsewhere, the president of the district immediately recommends a vacancy pastor and proposes a list of candidates from which the new pastor is elected and called. The vacancy pastor takes over all ministerial duties and helps the congregation extend the call for a new pastor. This is done in a meeting of the voting members. The congregation may add other names to the list submitted by the district president. After a ballot vote determines the choice of the man to be called, the vote is made unanimous by acclamation. The call is sent by registered or certified mail or delivered personally to the chosen candidate. In the case of a new mission, the district mission board selects the man and calls him.

The person who receives the call looks upon it as a "divine call"—one that has come to him from the Holy Spirit through a Christian congregation. Such a divine call brought him to the position he presently holds. Now he must decide, with the help of his congregation and with the aid of prayer and with the advice of his fellow pastors, whether he should keep the call he has or accept the new one. The procedure for calling a teacher is similar. The district president also proposes candidates with a statement of their qualifications, but it is the congregation that finds a substitute teacher during a classroom vacancy.

Members of congregations often take it for granted that there will always be pastors and teachers to serve them. But the questions arise: Where do pastors and teachers come from? Who were they before they became pastors and teachers? The answer is that they were boys and girls like those who are now in our Lutheran elementary schools. They came from Lutheran families located in small towns, in large cities or on farms. But before they could qualify as workers in the church, they had to spend long years in our worker training schools being educated and trained, especially learning the Word of God. They also learn how to preach, teach and share that Word and how to admonish and comfort young and old in the congregations. There is no quick and easy way into the full-time ministry of the church.

Need for Well-Trained Workers

Suppose some boy or girl today decides to prepare for full-time work in the church. Most people give thought to what they want to be someday: mechanics, nurses, teachers, ballplayers, computer programmers, astronauts or farmers. If a boy likes to read, is fond of his studies in school, learns rather easily and finds pleasure in learning his Bible history and catechism, then his pastor or teacher or parents may encourage him to study for the ministry. Sometimes the idea comes to him because of a sermon he heard or because of some remark he heard in school. Sometimes he gets the idea himself. But usually he was encouraged by someone who is interested in the work of the church and in the boy.

Once the decision has been made to prepare for the preaching or teaching ministry, the proper school has to be chosen. One of the first hard lessons our church learned soon after it was founded was that it would have to prepare its own pastors and teachers in its own schools if it hoped to survive. Today we have six synod schools that prepare our future pastors and teachers. In addition, the area Lutheran high schools offer programs that prepare students to enter our colleges.

Schools and Their Names

In former years private high schools and preparatory schools, like those at Mobridge, South Dakota, and New Ulm, Minnesota, were often called academies. When those two schools were closed and their operations were transferred to Prairie du Chien, Wisconsin, in 1979, the word "academy" was dropped. Both Martin Luther at Prairie du Chien and Northwestern at Watertown are now called preparatory schools. In our circles the synod schools are often called by the name of the city in which they are located. So we speak of graduating from Mequon or Saginaw, or of enrolling at Watertown or New Ulm.

The name "Northwestern" has an interesting history. When our young nation acquired the vast area between the Great Lakes and the Ohio River from England after the Revolutionary War, it became known as the Northwest Territory. Five states—Ohio, Indiana, Illinois, Michigan and Wisconsin—were carved out of it, and in each one "Northwest" or "Northwestern" became a popular name for institutions of all kinds. We still have a Northwestern Railroad, Northwestern University and Northwestern insurance companies. In our church a college and a preparatory school, a publishing house and a church paper bear the name "Northwestern." By a narrow margin it missed becoming the name of our synod at the time of the merger in 1917. The Rev. Carl Gausewitz, a prominent minister at that time, said: "We have a Northwestern College, a Northwestern Publishing House and a *Northwestern Lutheran*. Why not a Northwestern Synod?" But the majority of his colleagues voted in favor of naming it the "Joint Synod."

Two of our schools—at Mequon and Saginaw—are called seminaries. The original Latin word for seminary meant "seedplot" or "nursery," but in English it came to mean a school where pastors are trained. Though Saginaw is now a high school, it once was a real seminary. It retained the name to keep the past from being forgotten.

Dr. Martin Luther College got its rather long name because it was founded in 1883, exactly 400 years after Martin Luther was born in 1483. It was dedicated a year later on November 9, the day before Luther's birthday. In 1962, when the college and prep departments of DMLC were separated, it was natural that the prep school should retain the name of the great Reformer and become Martin Luther Academy. Then, when it was transferred to Prairie du Chien in 1979, the name went along, and the new school became Martin Luther Preparatory School.

Chapter 25

PREPARATORY SCHOOLS

Why We Have Preparatory Schools

The synod's main purpose in establishing and maintaining three preparatory schools is to provide pre-college training for boys and girls who plan to enter either the preaching or the teaching ministry. Courses at Northwestern Preparatory School are designed chiefly for those boys who intend to become pastors. Michigan Lutheran at Saginaw and Martin Luther at Prairie du Chien offer preparatory courses for both future pastors and teachers.

Subjects offered in all three "feeder" schools will naturally be more specialized than those in public high schools or even area Lutheran high schools, which cater to general students who do not plan to become full-time church workers. Most area Lutheran high schools, however, have departments in which students can take courses required for entry either into Northwestern College or Dr. Martin Luther College.

The courses of study at Martin Luther in Prairie du Chien will serve as an example of what is taught in our preparatory schools. All ninth grade pupils study religion and history, English, algebra and general science.

Those who intend to become pastors also study Latin and German. Those in the teachers' course must take piano lessons. This course also places greater emphasis on science, geography and music. The latest addition to the curriculum is the study of the Spanish language and culture.

Our preparatory schools have achieved their purpose if students do their work well, if their knowledge of God's Word has been increased, if their faith in their Savior has been strengthened and if they follow Christ the rest of their lives and serve him faithfully.

Northwestern — the Oldest Preparatory School

The oldest, continuously operated school in our church is Northwestern Preparatory School. It has existed since September of 1863. When the synod was about to open its first educational institution in that year in Watertown, it did not have a prep school in mind. Neither did President Bading when he told the synod that it must "dig a well" in its own country, in other words, establish a school to educate its own pastors. On his collection tour in Germany and Russia, President Bading asked Lutherans of

119

those countries to contribute funds for a new seminary, not a prep school.

What happened when the seminary was opened in September 1863? Three students appeared, but only one was a seminarian. The other two were local boys who wanted a high school education. Watertown at that time did not have a high school. During the next years other boys, including non-Lutherans, flocked to the new institution to take advantage of its high school program. In 1865, when the Lutheran college was founded and given the glamorous name of Northwestern University, all sixty-six students below the seminary level were enrolled in the first and second high-school classes. There were no collegians.

Six years later, however, there were eleven. But the number of preps had risen to 121. Seminarians left the Watertown school in 1870 because synod had decided to close the seminary. It had made arrangements with the Missouri Synod to have our theological students study at Concordia Seminary in St. Louis. The first college

Northwestern Campus

class of four did not graduate from Northwestern until 1872.

Up to the mid 1960s there have always been more preps than collegians at Northwestern. They lived together with collegians in one dormitory and called themselves students at Northwestern College rather than students in the preparatory department. All that changed in 1974 when the prep school began to be administered separately. Its name was changed to Northwestern Preparatory School, and Professor William Zell became its first president.

In the old days, when Northwestern "prep" was the only synodical "feeder" school, its dormitory served as a home away from home for hundreds of boys who came from faraway places in Wisconsin and neighboring states. Except for those who lived within walking or horse-and-buggy distance, the school dormitory was the only residence boys would know throughout the long school year. From the end of August to nearly the end of June, they had only a Christmas vacation to get home. No wonder that tears often flowed freely when a family said good-by for the first time to a young son and brother, who had made the noble resolve to study for the ministry at Northwestern University.

The young lad, who was probably filled with youthful enthusiasm and already pictured himself as a minister in his own church or as a missionary in "darkest Africa," was in for a number of surprises when he arrived at Northwestern. Instead of being a "university" student, he was only a humble ninth-grader, who in former years was subject to the discipline and sometimes unfriendly whims of upper classmen. For them he "shagged" (ran errands) and did other menial tasks. A ninth-grader and other lower classmen had to make the beds, sweep floors, lug in a pail of water every morning for washing hands and faces and then carry the waste water out again, clean and fill the kerosene lamps that supplied light at the large central study table, bring in wood from the woodpile for the stove in the study room, and carry out the ashes—the bedrooms were unheated. Actually the five boys in each room divided up these chores. Each boy would do them for a week and then be free until his turn came around again. The monitor's duty was to see that all the work was done promptly and efficiently.

Homesickness and hardships were soon forgotten in the round of activities. The boys had five hours of classes each morning, including Saturdays, two hours of study in the afternoon and again in the evening, two free hours in the afternoon, and three short chapel devotions every day except Sunday (after breakfast, at the beginning of classes, and at bedtime). On Sundays the whole student body marched to church at St. Mark.

Besides all this, there were new friends, new teachers and new studies, such as Latin and Greek. Many students, finding the languages too difficult, dropped out. But for those who stayed, each new course brought new horizons. There were sports and other recreations. In the 1880s, football was played like soccer. Thirty or forty could play on a side, and sides were chosen from boys who came out to watch the game. A boy could join the military company, or, if he was musical, the band or orchestra. During the winter he could practice gymnastics or take part in military drills in the old wooden gym. In spring there was baseball, and all year long those not athletically inclined took long hikes within the city or far out into the country. Swimming in the Rock River and skating on its ice in the winter were also popular forms of exercise.

In 1905 the standard of living rose measurably for Northwestern students when they moved into a new dormitory that had steam heating, electric lights, indoor plumbing and showers. About that time, the modern game of football became popular, and tennis was added to the roster of sports. In 1912, when a group of former students in Milwaukee raised enough money to build a fine new gymnasium, basketball became a favorite sport. That gymnasium is now the auditorium—the oldest building on the campus.

In recent years the preparatory school has undergone many changes. Campus buildings now are modern, attractive and functional. There are new sports—wrestling, track, cross country—and more interscholastic competitions. Students publish a school paper, the *Hornet*, and each senior class produces a yearbook, the *Sprinter*. Students have opportunities to take part in band and choruses and

Northwestern Gymnasium

in forensics and drama. The "Prep Singers" have won high praise for their concerts at home and on tour. Pastor Mark G. Schroeder has succeeded Prof. Zell as president.

The essentials at Northwestern have not changed. The preparatory school has never lost sight of its primary goal to provide a solid foundation of spiritual and secular knowledge for those who plan to enter the service of the church. Faculty members help students become adjusted to the new life and try to keep them motivated so that the four years spent at school will remain among the most influential and enjoyable of their lives. Here, in a congenial Christian environment, the slightly bewildered ninth-graders are transformed into the dedicated young men and women who receive their diplomas on gradua-

tion day. A high percentage of them will enter college to continue their preparation for becoming full-time workers in the church.

Michigan Lutheran Seminary

The early history of the Michigan Synod has already been briefly told. Michigan Lutherans had the same problems as those in Wisconsin, and for some years they had to depend almost entirely on pastors who drifted into the state from Germany. Among them were many unfaithful, ignorant men who, by their lives and teachings, brought disgrace upon the Michigan Synod and did it great harm.

Finally, more than twenty years after the Wisconsin Synod had opened its seminary, Michigan, under the leadership of its able president, Christoph Eberhardt, resolved to educate its own men in a school of its own. Rev. Alex Lange, of Remus, Michigan, a former seminary teacher in Buffalo, agreed to serve as professor, besides doing the work in his parish. A few young men were willing to prepare for the ministry, and in 1885 Pastor Lange began teaching them.

About that time he accepted a call to Manchester, Michigan, in Washtenaw County, where a member of the congregation offered the use of a two-story brick building for the seminary. The Michigan Synod voted to accept the offer. It extended a call to Pastor Lange to be the full-time professor, and in 1886 he opened the school with six students. Two of the six were Fred Krauss and John Westendorf. Both of these men—and a son of each one after him—served as presidents of the Michigan District.

The building in Manchester had been offered for use for only two years. So the Michigan Synod had to decide where to establish its school permanently. Saline, Adrian and Saginaw were all considered. President Eber-

Port of Saginaw along the Saginaw River
Picture, courtesy The Saginaw News

hardt decided the vote in favor of Saginaw. He also donated almost four acres for the site, drew plans for the "Old Main" building, and made liberal donations for construction and equipment. Even the old seminary bell was his gift to the school. Besides all this, he served the school as professor when his services were needed. Pastor Eberhardt is justly called "The Father of Michigan Lutheran Seminary."

The new seminary was dedicated on September 20, 1887. On the next day classes began with fourteen students in attendance. Alex Lange was the president and the only full-time professor. He also served as dormitory overseer, athletic director and school janitor.

The course of study was to cover seven years, but very few students remained in school that long. The first two graduates must have been older men who had had a great deal of previous education, because they were declared ready for the pastoral ministry at the close of the first year, graduating on July 28, 1888. President Lange remained at the school only one year after it was moved to Saginaw. Rev. F. Huber succeeded him as president, followed in 1893 by Prof. Otto Hoyer of New Ulm. Hoyer headed the institution only two years before accepting a call to Northwestern College in 1895.

The years following 1893 were troubled ones for the Michigan Synod and its seminary. Many Michigan pastors opposed forming the federated Joint Synod in 1893 and, moreover, opposed closing their seminary and reducing it to the rank of a high school. Synod President Eberhardt did not favor this idea either, but he yielded, and the theological department was closed for one year. After his death in 1893, it was reopened, and in 1896 Michigan withdrew from the Joint Synod.

The seminary continued under two succeeding presidents but went rapidly downhill after 1902. At the end of the school year of 1907, it had only one student, so the board decided to close the school, thus ending the first period of its history. For three years the only person on the premises was the faithful caretaker, Mrs. May, who had served as housekeeper since 1896 and remained in service at the school until 1932.

In 1909, at the convention of the Joint Synod in Fort Atkinson, Wisconsin, the Michigan Synod again applied for membership in the federation. It agreed to reopen its "seminary" as a four-year high school and to use the colleges at Watertown and New Ulm for the further education of those who wished to become pastors and teachers.

The new board of control decided to reopen the school in 1910 with one class, the ninth grade, and one professor, who was also to be the president. Rev. O. J. R. Hoenecke of Milwaukee accepted the call to that position and remained director of the seminary until 1950, when he asked to be relieved of the duties of the presidency. He continued to serve as teacher until his retirement in 1960.

A new era in the history of the school began on September 13, 1910, with about twenty-five persons attending opening exercises. Three boys and a girl had enrolled. But within a year a second class was added, and a second professor, Adolf Sauer, was called to join Director Hoenecke. Since then the school has grown steadily. The first group of MLS graduates entered Northwestern College in 1914. Of those one died of tuberculosis while at the Wauwatosa Seminary, three became ministers, and one, Theodore Binhammer, served as professor of mathematics at Northwestern for nearly half a century.

The expansion of the school required more buildings: in 1951, an administration building; in 1954, a new dining hall; in 1963, a student union; in 1976, a new double dormitory large enough to accommodate 350 boys and girls. In the 1980s the school worked energetically to complete its masterplan for the entire campus. In particular, the cafeteria was moved to the lower level of the dormitory, a new gymnasium was built to accommodate athletic programs for both male and female students, the old gymnasium was converted to a chapel-auditorium, and the former dining hall was incorporated into offices and a student union which joined the dormitory and the academic center. In the course of all this construction, Old Main, the impressive landmark of the school for eighty years, had to be razed.

Professor Conrad Frey was president of MLS from 1950 to 1966, when he succeeded Prof. C. Schweppe as

president of Dr. Martin Luther College. Prof. Martin Toepel held the office for the next twelve years until his retirement. In 1978 Pastor John C. Lawrenz was named president.

Martin Luther Preparatory School

After more than a year of deliberations, the Wisconsin Synod in a special session in 1978 resolved to buy the beautiful 108-acre campus of Campion Jesuit High School in Prairie du Chien, Wisconsin, for its new preparatory school. Enrollment at the Roman Catholic institution had been dwindling steadily and the Jesuites were offering to sell the property at a fraction of its real value.

Our church, because of crowded conditions at New Ulm, had faced the necessity of building an entirely new prep school to accommodate Martin Luther Academy either at New Ulm or elsewhere. The plan was to combine the Northwestern Lutheran Academy of Mobridge and possibly the Northwestern Preparatory school in Watertown with the new school on a new campus. But the cost of such an institution, running to ten or twelve million dollars, seemed prohibitive.

That was the situation when the Jesuit school became available. The chief argument against the purchase was that Campion lay too far from the center of our Lutheran population and that parents would not send their children so far away from home. Some also thought that the bargain price of just under three million dollars (plus an extra million to adapt the buildings to our needs, build professorages and move the equipment from New Ulm and Mobridge) was too high in a time of inflation, when the shortage of money called for retrenchment rather than spending.

first years. With a song in their hearts and praise to God, they compared the new school to "a tree planted by the waters and spreading its roots by the river."

Excitement filled the air as 362 students—170 boys and 192 girls—from twenty-six states and Canada registered on opening day, September 4, 1979. One hundred fifty-one had come

MLPS Athletic Center and swimming pool

But the arguments in favor of the purchase won the day. Here was a spacious campus with eight major, beautifully appointed buildings, including a new gymnasium with an Olympic-sized indoor swimming pool, that would fill the needs for more space in our preparatory school system and at the college in New Ulm for many years. Such an opportunity might not come again. Surely God had provided an answer to prayers.

Once the decision to purchase had been made, people all over the synod eagerly awaited reports of the first enrollment. The happy results can be gauged from the report of the new board of control of the school for the

from Martin Luther Academy and sixty from Northwestern at Mobridge. Eighteen professors, one tutor and one housemother had also joined the exodus from these schools to the banks of the Mississippi. Rev. Oscar Siegler, president at MLA, continued as pres-

Girl's Dormitory, MLPS

ident of the new school to aid in the transition. Of the total number of students, ninety-nine were enrolled in the pastors', 237 in the teachers' and twenty-six in the general course.

There were regrets over the closing of the school at Mobridge, after it had served as an outpost of Lutheran education in the Dakota-Montana District for fifty years. But they were forgotten at the joyful dedication of the new school on Sunday, October 12, 1979. God had blessed this venture of faith on the part of the synod, and its members were duly grateful.

The school was on its way. In the second year the enrollment was 351 and the faculty numbered thirty, including part-time instructors. The synod decided to hold its biennial convention on the campus in August 1981. In 1982 Rev. Theodore B. Olsen succeeded Pastor Siegler as president.

There was every reason to believe that the tree planted by the waters of a great river would serve in guiding more and more young people toward the goal of becoming full-time laborers in the Lord's kingdom as pastors and teachers.

Following such promising beginnings, however, Martin Luther Preparatory School had to face some hard times too. By its tenth year, the total enrollment had dwindled to 218 students. Nevertheless, in that same year the school dedicated a new music hall and noted that it was still providing a significant number of students for continued training for the full-time ministry. In nine years, 121 students had gone from the prep school to the pastors' course at Northwestern College and 216 to the teachers' course at Dr. Martin Luther College.

Chapter 26

DR. MARTIN LUTHER COLLEGE

Founder, Rev. C. J. Albrecht

Rev. C. J. Albrecht

The founder of Dr. Martin Luther College was Rev. C. J. Albrecht, pastor of St. Paul's congregation in New Ulm and president of the old Minnesota Synod. In 1871 that synod had decided to send its young men to Northwestern College and agreed to furnish one professor for the faculty there. But the plan could not be carried out because the Minnesota Synod lacked the money to pay even one man's salary. The whole state of Minnesota had been hit hard by crop failures because of a grasshopper plague.

By 1883 the Minnesota Synod was recovering from financial setbacks, but it still suffered from a shortage of pastors. Pastor Albrecht was convinced that more young men might be persuaded to study for the ministry if they could attend a school nearby instead of having to go to distant Watertown for their schooling. In its 1883 convention the Minnesota Synod agreed with him and resolved to found a college that should bear Martin Luther's name, because its founding marked the quadricentennial of Luther's birth. Pastor Albrecht's congregation promised to donate the necessary land and $5,000 in cash. That was why New Ulm, Minnesota, was chosen to be the site of the new institution.

New Ulm

New Ulm is about 100 miles southwest of the Twin Cities. A city of some 15,000 people, it lies in a picturesque valley created by two rivers that come together there, the Minnesota and the Cottonwood. From a wooded bluff in its west central section, the campus of Dr. Martin Luther College overlooks the city.

In a state usually thought of as a stronghold of Norwegians and Swedes, New Ulm is unusual, having been settled by Germans and still being quite German in character. It took its name from the city of Ulm in Germany, and its former post office, now a museum, is said to be the copy of a public building in Ulm. Children in New Ulm used to talk to each other in German on the streets. Clerks in stores could understand and speak German. Some still do. But the New Ulm speech was not pure German, and it was far from being pure English. It was rather an interesting mixture of the two languages.

New Ulm was probably the last city of any size to undergo an Indian massacre. In 1862 the Sioux went on the warpath, attacked the town, killed twenty-six people and burned 190 houses. New Ulmers still point out spots on an old building where bullets left their marks. Historic markers of the event are located throughout the city.

DMLC'S "OLD MAIN"

On June 25, 1884, Dr. Martin Luther College laid the cornerstone of its first building, "Old Main." That day is precious to the Lutheran church because on June 25 in 1530 the Augsburg Confession was read before the diet (parliament) of the German nation in the city of Augsburg. Old Main, patterned after the old Concordia Seminary in St. Louis, was dedicated on November 9, and the first classes were held in it the next day, November 10, Luther's birthday.

For the next twenty-five years, Old Main and a small structure called the "turnhall" comprised the entire physical plant of the college. Not until 1909 did the school add a boys' dormitory

Old Main, DMLC

and a music hall to the campus. Today DMLC's Old Main, with its high Gothic windows and its slender tower surmounted by a cross, still stands tall among a complex of newer and larger buildings.

Within one year after the opening of Dr. Martin Luther College, the school had eighty students. Like Northwestern College, it was at first mainly a high school, with a preparatory and an academic department. High school students outnumbered all others even when a theological department was added in 1885 and a teachers' course in 1886. The school at one time had six different departments. By the time the synods of Wisconsin, Minnesota and Michigan formed the federated General or Joint Synod in 1892, DMLC had graduated thirty pastors and eight teachers and provided an academic and commercial training for a large number of others.

Normal School

In the federation of 1892, each synod remained an independent unit, retaining its real estate and other properties and being responsible for its debts. The synods did agree, however, to turn over the operation of their schools to the Joint Synod, and that body decided that one seminary, Wisconsin Lutheran, and one college, Northwestern, would be enough for preparing pastors. Dr. Martin Luther College would be a normal school, its main purpose being to educate teachers for the synod's parish schools. At the same time it was to serve as a preparatory school for those who wished to become pastors. So it became the second of the "feeders"—after Northwestern Prep—annually sending graduates from the prep department to Northwestern College. DMLC also continued to offer courses for those who desired only a general education.

The college began to operate as a normal school in 1893. In the following decades it added new subject matter to the teachers' course but required only one year of college until 1920, when a second year was added. A third year was added some years later, and in the early 1950s DMLC became a full-fledged, four-year college. In 1980 it received full accreditation with the North Central Association of Colleges.

In 1896 the synod decided to make the school coeducational, and two years later the first girl, Miss Lillie Mohr, graduated from the normal department. At first only a few young women enrolled, but by 1925 their number equaled and in recent decades exceeded the number of young men in attendance.

Prof. Carl L. Schweppe

The first president of the school was Pastor C. J. Albrecht. It was Carl L. Schweppe, its president from 1934 to 1966, however, who helped to establish it as a four-year college. He was succeeded in 1966 by Pastor Conrad I. Frey, former president of Michigan Lutheran Seminary. President Frey retired June 30, 1980, having served during the period of the college's greatest growth in student enrollment, faculty and facilities. Also during his tenure the school undertook a faculty self-study leading to accreditation. Professor Lloyd Huebner, who had

Student Union

been vice-president of student affairs, succeeded Conrad Frey as president of the college.

The four acres donated by St. Paul's congregation in 1883 have been expanded into a parklike fifty-acre campus with eleven major buildings, including male and female residence halls, a fine library, a music center, and the Luther Memorial Union. Luther Memorial, the largest building on the campus, contains a well-appointed student union on its upper level and a kitchen and cafeteria below. To the rear is a spacious gymnasium with accommodations that allow it to be used as an auditorium. Older buildings have undergone extensive renovations. Old Main is now the administration building. The former administration building, built in 1928, is the Academic Center, containing a 900-seat chapel-auditorium.

Curriculum

Like all our schools, Dr. Martin Luther College bases its teaching on the solid foundation of the Word of God and centers its entire campus life on the gospel of Jesus Christ. For that reason the curriculum places the proper emphasis on courses in Bible study and religion. Chapel services are a part of every-day life. Since the school prepares future teachers for our synod's Lutheran elementary school system, the major emphasis of the curriculum is elementary education. This program reaches its climax in the senior year with a professional semester, during which the student does practice teaching under the guidance of a college supervisor either in an elementary school in New Ulm or in other elementary schools of the synod.

Organ in Chapel-Auditorium, DMLC

History is also emphasized, since this provides the background against which God's plan of salvation has been and is carried out among the nations of the world. More recently science and mathematics, too, have received increased attention in order to provide the necessary background for our synod's teachers in the modern world. Because the Lutheran church has always rejoiced in its rich musical heritage and because many teachers direct church choirs and play the organ for church services, piano and organ instruction and music courses are stressed. Teaching involves commun-

131

icating with others. Thus, speech, composition and literature courses also make up an important part of the curriculum.

In 1988 DMLC expanded its curriculum to include preparation for secondary education. Students wanting the secondary program must take a fifth year of study to complete it. At graduation, however, their first calls are usually to the Lutheran elementary schools.

Like all our synodical schools, DMLC also has a well-rounded program of athletics and extracurricular activities designed to keep its students healthy and happy.

after the daily routine of studies is forgotten. Such are the homecoming, the snow carnival, the concerts, the annual play and the musical. The most memorable of all the highlights is the Christmas season because it is the hallowed time of our Savior's birth. Decorations made by the students then adorn the halls of the Academic Center, the rooms of the residence halls and the outside of campus buildings. Everything reaches its climax in the Christmas concert presented just prior to the Christmas recess.

For seniors a highlight occurs just prior to their graduation. At that time in May the synodical Assignment

Centennial Hall

Highlights

Student life at DMLC is not without its special events and festivities—highlights—that are remembered long

Committee meets on campus to assign graduates to their first schools. The two days of assignment activities culminate on the second day when the graduates are informed of their assigned calls.

A few days later, during the graduation service, each graduate is awarded the Bachelor of Science in Education degree. Immediately after the recessional the graduates receive the actual calls extended to them by congregations. All this represents the end result of many years of hard work, the fulfillment of a desire and the attainment of a goal—service in the Lord's kingdom, the greatest highlight of all.

A familiar sight from the city of New Ulm, as one looks up to the DMLC campus, is the lighted tower of Old Main, standing majestically against a clear, starry sky. As the light shines forth every night, it is the prayer of every member of our church that the graduates who step forth from the halls of DMLC into the classrooms of our Lutheran schools will be a light unto others, even as Christ, the Light of their lives, shines into the lives of the students before them and into the lives of the world about them.

Old Main and Music Center at night

Chapter 27

NORTHWESTERN COLLEGE

President Adam Martin

Much of the early history of Northwestern College has already been told in connection with the story of its education twin, Northwestern Preparatory School. Both Northwesterns have, from their beginnings, shared the same campus. In former days they were looked upon as a single institution rather than as two separate schools.

The name "university," given to the college by its first president, Rev. Adam Martin, did not seem as unusual in 1865 as it does today. Church

Prof. Adam Martin

organizations all over the Midwest were founding colleges and universities on a shoestring in those days, and some grew to be large institutions that are still with us.

President Martin had a vision of a great Lutheran university, "equal to any in the land," with faculties of law, medicine, and art, as well as theology. Though he understood that his primary purpose was to prepare a Lutheran ministry, he also wanted to serve the community and raise the cultural level of German immigrants. He felt that they were being treated as inferiors and that his university should help to teach them "to take their merited position in public life."

Martin's enthusiasm seems to have inspired both college trustees and synodical leaders for a time. They heartily endorsed his plan of raising an endowment fund of $100,000 by selling perpetual scholarships at $500 apiece. Each one guaranteed the buyer and his heirs free tuition at Northwestern for all time. Martin's lofty ideas were reechoed by D. W. Ballou, editor of the Watertown *Democrat*, who urged local citizens to "carry forward this noble enterprise to a successful conclusion and make Watertown preeminent for its schools and college."

Watertown

Situated about halfway between Milwaukee and the state capital, Madison, Watertown was once the second largest city in Wisconsin. It lost that distinction when the plank road that connected it with Milwaukee deteriorated and the railways extended their lines beyond the city to the west. The first settlers were "Yankees" from New York state. Germans arrived in great numbers after 1842, and the Irish followed soon after. An old surveyor used to say that he directed Americans to the south, the Irish to the west and the Germans to the central part of the city. To some extent these divisions are still discernible.

Most numerous among the Germans were the Lutherans. Today the town has seven Lutheran congregations, four affiliated with the Wisconsin Synod. In the early days a small but influential group of "48-ers," (people who fled from Germany after the unsuccessful revolution there in 1848) arrived in the city. They were educated people but had to resort to humble occupations and farming and were therefore called Latin farmers. Most prominent among them was Carl Schurz, who became a Civil War general and Secretary of the Interior under President R. B. Hayes. His wife, Margarethe, opened the first kindergarten in America in Watertown in 1856.

In 1865 Watertown was chosen as the site of Northwestern College, partly because "it was surrounded by farming communities that would furnish food for the tables and because conditions in a small town were more favorable to education than those in a large city."

President August F. Ernst

When President Martin's plan to create an endowment fund failed, he proposed that the college be removed to Milwaukee—the high school was to remain in Watertown—and that wealthy Milwaukeeans be approached to pledge $25,000 for the necessary buildings. But German Lutherans were in no position to finance such an undertaking, nor were they in the mood "to take their merited position in public life," so outsiders did not respond with cash. Disappointed in his hopes, Martin resigned early in 1869, returned to the East and became professor of German at Gettsyburg College until his retirement in 1898. He died at eight-six in 1921 in New Haven, Connecticut. He had a pleasing personality and outstanding oratorical ability, but his views on education and theology were hopelessly at odds with the growing confessionalism in our church. Martin's successor was Prof. Lewis O. Thompson, who served as president of the college for only one year.

In the meantime, financial affairs worsened, and by 1870 the school was ready to close its doors for want of money. The trustees sold part of their thirty-acre property and mortgaged the remainder not only once but three times to meet obligations. At last synod President Bading made a heartfelt appeal to the congregations to come to the support of their school. They responded favorably and Northwestern was saved.

Our church was blessed in the choice of a replacement for both Martin and Thompson. It called Rev. August F. Ernst, a vigorous man of twenty-eight and a staunch Lutheran, who had received an excellent university education in Germany. He had migrated to this country in 1863 and served as a pastor in the East. Two years after arriving in Watertown, he was called to be president—or director, which was also the title in those days—of the college. He held that office for nearly 50 years, until 1919. With the coming of Pastor Ernst, a new chapter in Northwestern's history began. He soon remodeled the school after a German "gymnasium," or pre-university school, a pattern it kept until the American college and high school system was introduced in 1920.

Prof. August Ernst

Curiously, the name "university" lingered on, even though Northwestern had dropped its seminary department in 1870 and its teacher training school in 1893. In that year it also considered and rejected an offer to combine with a medical school from Milwaukee. Finally, in 1910 Northwestern University became Northwestern College, a name that suited it better.

Through Ernst's influence it also became what it was originally intended to be—a preministerial school for students planning to enter Wisconsin Lutheran Seminary. In the 1870s that meant that German would be the medium of instruction, since most of the people in our congregations still spoke German and attended German services. In his efforts to serve the community President Martin had tried to make it an English college. Many of the students with English and Irish names now left the school. The enrollment plummeted. The introduction of the teachers' course in 1876 and later on a business course helped to bring some of it back.

In 1919, the year after World War I ended, Rev. Erwin E. Kowalke succeeded Ernst as president of Northwestern. In that year the transition to English began when one half of the beginners were getting their Latin by means of English in a "parallel class." The other half still understood enough German to learn their Latin through German. The change to English as a medium of instruction was completed in the late thirties, the Hebrew classes being the last holdouts. By that time most of the services in the synod were conducted in English.

Prof. Erwin E. Kowalke

President Martin sometimes appointed men of other religious denominations as professors at Northwestern. Prof. Lewis Thompson, a fine gentleman and a sincere man, was a Presbyterian. Since 1883 the entire faculty has been Lutheran. Throughout its history the college proper has been mainly a school for men, though no girl was ever refused admittance if she cared to take the rigorous classical course planned mainly for future ministers. Twenty-two girls accepted this challenge and received their B.A.'s between 1896 and 1968. Only two or three have enrolled for a year in the college since then.

Extracurricular Activities

From the beginning Northwestern had a strong faith in the Latin proverb *Mens sana in corpore sano* (a healthy mind dwells in a healthy body). Sawing wood for stoves in each room provided healthful exercise before the era of central heating and was often applied as punishment for infractions of rules. Jogging around the campus was popular a century before it became a fad in our time. In the 1870s students built their own wooden gym to have a place for games, gymnastics and military drill during the winter months. Every autumn, since long before the turn of the century, the athletic field has been crowded with football players—most training for the varsity and other teams, but some just out for fun and exercise. Though no efforts were ever made to recruit or subsidize players, Northwestern teams have won their share of victories, and in one period during the early 1950s remained undefeated for four consecutive years. When classes ran into the middle of June, baseball was a more prominent

sport than it is today, when the season is cut short because of the early school closing.

After a new gym was built in 1912, basketball became the most popular indoor sport, and still remains so. Both the college and the preparatory school host tournaments for Lutheran elementary and high schools, as measures of student recruitment and good will. Recently soccer, tennis, wrestling, golf and track teams have entered intercollegiate competition along with football, basketball and baseball.

Long before Northwestern had a regular music department, the German Lutheran love of music was much in evidence, not least in the singing and organ playing in chapel services. The college has had a band and a male chorus since the 1880s and an orchestra during much of that time, besides vocal quartettes and instrumental combos of all kinds. A touring chorus carries the message of the gospel in song to congregations in annual tours.

Programs of literary societies, providing both entertainment and practice in speaking for students, have been features of college life almost from the beginning. Today the Forum Society, a dramatic organization, stages an annual play or musical. The *Black and Red* has been the respected literary magazine of the college for more than ninety years, and since 1970 each senior class publishes a yearbook, *Mnema*.

Northwestern Today

A construction project that began in the early 1950s and ended in the middle 1970s has virtually created a new campus. All the old buildings are gone except the gymnasium of 1912, and that has been transformed into an auditorium, which now also houses the music department. Instead of one dormitory, there are now three residence halls to accommodate the increased enrollment.

Gone are the days when preps had to mow the lawns and shovel the walks in winter. The thirty-eight-acre campus is now under the care of a custodial staff. Administrative duties, which were either non-existent in the old days or attended to by one or two faculty members, are in this more complex age performed increasingly by professional staff personnel. A professional chef is in charge of the school cafeteria.

Even the curriculum has undergone changes. Electives were introduced for the first time in the upper classes in 1961. Class hours—recitations—have been reduced in number, and more stress has been placed on independent study. Yet the course still consists mainly of classical and liberal arts studies. A knowledge of biblical languages, Greek and Hebrew, and to a lesser extent, German and Latin, is still considered essential for the education of men who are going to occupy our pulpits and "labor in the Word and doctrine."

More attention is given to the orientation of incoming freshmen and to their motivation later on. Counseling has become an adjunct to teaching. "Ministry convocations"—lectures on specific aspects of the Lutheran min-

NWC Wittenberg Dormitory

NWC Chapel-Arts Building

NWC Chapel

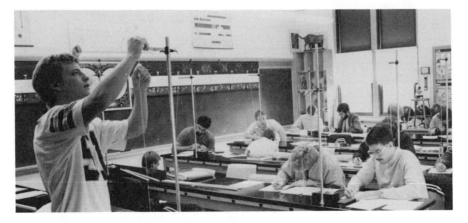

NWC Science Classroom

istry by visiting pastors—are regularly scheduled for the students and are much appreciated by them.

During the 1970s the faculty explored conditions necessary for accreditation with the North Central Association of Colleges. In 1981 Northwestern College received accreditation with this association.

In his commencement addresses, Dr. Ernst often spoke of the college as a *"Werkstaette des Heiligen Geistes"*—a place where the work of the Holy Spirit is being done. His successors in the presidency—Erwin E. Kowalke (1919-1959), Carleton Toppe (1959-1987) and Robert J. Voss (1987-)—have not only held to this stated purpose but enlarged it and made it more explicit.

It does not mean that Northwestern is a cloistered community apart from the world. The college uses secular textbooks, graduate studies in the world's universities, tax exemption and student aids from the world's governments, and accreditation from a worldly association. Yet its guiding purpose since the days of the founders has always been to share in the work of the Spirit and to prepare young men for their high calling as ministers of Jesus Christ.

Chapter 28

WISCONSIN LUTHERAN SEMINARY

Seminary Student

Probably no student enrolls at the seminary without in some measure feeling the truth expressed by the psalmist: "Since my youth, O God, you have taught me, and to this day I declare your marvelous deeds" (71:17). Behind the enrolling student lie as many as eight long years of education in God's Word. The four seminary years will seem more like a fulfillment or a great new experience, rather than a mere continuation of what he has already received. Every course taught here will have a practical bearing on his future profession.

The pastoral life really begins at the seminary. At the end of his first year

Chancel of the Chapel

the student will be ready to accept invitations to preach. In his third year he will serve as a vicar in a congregation under the guidance of an experienced pastor. Before entering the seminary, he was a member of the flock. Now he will be educated to be a shepherd to whom Christ still says, as he did to Peter: "Feed my lambs. Feed my sheep."

Seminary work is also different in other ways. Though grades are still given in examinations and on written assignments, the emphasis is rather on each student's faithful use of his particular gifts and talents. No report cards are issued, even though records are kept to make transcripts of academic credits available at any time for future graduate work.

In the seminary the student puts to use the knowledge he has acquired in high school and college. He studies the Bible in the languages in which it was first written—the Old Testament in Hebrew, the New Testament in Greek—so that he may be sure that he preaches God's Word as God meant it to be preached. He practices writing and speaking and learns how a sermon should be prepared and delivered.

Biblical doctrines are studied in depth, and much attention is given to

Entrance to Library

naries in this country. In its first year, 1863, it started out with one professor, Dr. Edward Moldehnke, and one theological student in a private residence in Watertown. In that year President Lincoln proclaimed the freedom of Negro slaves, the battle of Gettysburg was fought and the President delivered his famous address over the graves of the fallen. The battle raged near the site of the Gettysburg Seminary, from which a number of pastors had come to serve our synod. That seminary at Gettysburg served as Gen. Robert E. Lee's headquarters during the battle.

church history. A student also learns how to share the Word, how he ought to conduct himself in the ministry, how to comfort the sick, how to reprove the wrongdoers, how to instruct the children and, especially in recent years, how to discuss the problems of troubled parishioners in private consultations and help them to arrive at God-pleasing solutions. The pastor does not speak his own wisdom, but he proclaims God's truth, following the Lord's admonition: " . . . let the one who has my word speak it faithfully" (Jeremiah 23:28).

Early Years of the Seminary

Today Wisconsin Lutheran Seminary (WLS) is among the larger semi-

Prof. E. Moldehnke

After a year, Dr. Moldehnke and his seminarians moved to St. Mark's parish school, where they remained until the synod's first college, known briefly as Wisconsin University and then

142

as Northwestern University, was founded in 1865. For the next five years the seminary operated in Northwestern's Old Main, the "coffee mill," its third home. Rev. Adolf Hoenecke was called to be the professor of theology when Dr. Moldehnke returned to Germany in 1866. Twelve pastors finished their studies at the seminary in those first years in Watertown.

In 1870 the students of the theological department were transferred to Concordia Seminary in St. Louis as the result of an agreement with the Missouri Synod to conduct a joint seminary. Among Wisconsin Synod men who studied at St. Louis were John P. Koehler, later professor and director of Wisconsin Lutheran Seminary, and three Pieper brothers: Franz, who became president of Concordia Seminary and the ranking theologian of the Missouri Synod; Reinhold, later president of Springfield Seminary; and August, a longtime professor and president at WLS. Twenty-one Wisconsin Synod pastors received their training at St. Louis.

In 1878 our church reopened its seminary in two small dwellings in Milwaukee. Adolf Hoenecke again became its head while also retaining his pastorate at St. Matthew for another nine years. The synod soon bought a small park at 13th and Vine streets for $9,500 and converted the hall on the property into the sixth home of the seminary. It was on these grounds that the first area Lutheran high school was located in 1903. During the fifteen Milwaukee years, 121 pastors graduated from the seminary.

Seminary in Wauwatosa

An important milestone in synodical history was reached in 1892 with the forming of a federation of the three synods of Wisconsin, Minnesota and Michigan. As a result of increased enrollment, a new and larger seminary building was erected on a small lot of land about half the size of a city block at 60th and Lloyd streets in Wauwatosa. The total cost, including three professorages, was $38,600. The move into this rather handsome Victorian building was the seventh for the seminary. Dedication followed in September 1893. Prof. Hoenecke continued as administrator, succeeded by Prof. Koehler in 1920. During the next thirty-six years 493 seminarians were taught the "Wauwatosa Gospel" in this building. (See page 60.) Many considered this period a golden age of the seminary.

Eighth Home of the Seminary

The time came when the school outgrew its home in Wauwatosa. The grounds were not large enough for expansion, so the synod purchased an eighty-acre farm in Mequon, about fifteen miles north of Milwaukee, as

143

Seminary Tower

the site of a new seminary. Construction began immediately on a complex of buildings designed to resemble the Wartburg, the German castle where Luther translated the New Testament into German. After the dedication in 1929, the seminary moved into its eighth home, and Prof. August Pieper began the first of his eight years as president.

A visitor is impressed with the sturdiness of the WLS buildings. When the old barn standing on the farm site was torn down, some of the hand-hewn timbers were saved and used in the construction of the seminary chapel, where they can still be seen today. A large entrance tower dominates the campus. It contains the room well known to our synod's pastors for five decades as the place where they were assigned their first calls into the pastoral ministry by the synodical Assignment Committee. The tower divides the large C-shaped building into two areas: the dining and residence halls to the west and an administration-classroom building, chapel and library to the east.

In recent years the seminary has grown both in enrollment and in the size of its physical plant. In 1929 four professors' homes were built on the grounds. Twelve more have been added since then. Residence halls, originally designed for seventy-two students, have been enlarged to accommodate 126. A new dining hall, twice the size of the original, seats 250 students. The original four teaching stations have been increased to nine. In 1968 a splendid new library with a capacity of 75,000 volumes was dedicated. In addition to the library proper, it contains well-lighted, air-conditioned areas for study, offices for the library staff, lounges for faculty and students, and a multipurpose assembly room capable of seating up to 100 persons. This assembly room is suit-

Seminary gymnasium

able for classes, seminars, conferences and audio-visual presentations. In 1986 a new auditorium-gymnasium was constructed apart from the C-shaped building. The former gymnasium was subsequently converted to classrooms and space for the synod archives.

In the years at Mequon, the seminary has enjoyed the services of six presidents. Prof. John P. Meyer succeeded August Pieper in 1937, followed by E. Reim (1954-1957), Carl Lawrenz (1957-1978), Armin Schuetze (1978-1985) and Armin Panning (1985-).

In an average year about one-third of the seminarians are married and live off-campus.

The seminary at Mequon, situated on a large and beautifully wooded tract of land in the midst of a choice residential area is as close to the center of our synod as it is possible to be. It seems unlikely that it will ever have to move again.

Synodical Assignment Committee

After a student graduates from the seminary, he is ready to enter the actual work of the pastoral ministry. Who decides where he will begin his work? In business and industry a college graduate may go out and look for a job to his liking, or he may choose from a number of jobs offered him. His choice may be determined by the salary offered, the working conditions, the opportunity for promotions or the nearness to his home. Our pastor graduates do not choose the area, town or church where they will serve. Nor do they receive their first call directly from a congregation. They are given their first call through the synodical Assignment Committee.

Seminary graduates may be assigned as pastors to self-supporting congregations, to mission congregations or new mission fields, or as in-

structors in synodical schools or area Lutheran high schools. These men willingly and gratefully accept their calls because they believe that the Holy Spirit is leading them to their place of work through the Assignment Committee. They say to their Lord and Savior: "Here am I, send me."

The Assignment Committee consists of the president of the synod and the presidents of the synodical districts. Also present at the assignment meetings are the president and several professors of the seminary, the presidents of synodical schools, and administrators for various boards, who serve in an advisory capacity. These men have before them information on the abilities, qualifications and interests of each of the graduates and also the requests from the various congregations and schools for candidates to serve them as pastors and teachers.

After a careful and prayerful consideration of the requirements of the calls and the qualifications of the candidates, the district presidents vote on the assignment of each candidate, the object being to place the right man in the right place. After the work of the Assignment Committee is finished, the formal calls are handed to the young pastors in a public service. They then have the opportunity to meet with the district presidents to be more fully informed about the conditions, challenges and responsibilities of their prospective charges.

Other Training Schools for Pastors

Our seminary in Mequon is not the only school in our church which educates future pastors and missionaries. We and the national churches have also established seminaries in Central Africa, Japan, Hong Kong, El Paso in Texas and Colombia in South America; the last two train Spanish-speaking pastors. In July 1971 the first World Mission Seminary Conference was held in Hong Kong. Since then there have been other conferences at which representatives from all the seminaries met to strengthen one another, so that the truth is preserved as we share it with the world.

Beginning in 1962 our church had an arrangement with Bethany Lutheran College of the Evangelical Lutheran Synod, Mankato, Minnesota. Bethany College agreed to provide pre-seminary training for men of our church over twenty-one years of age, and especially married men, who did not have the necessary college background. This "Bethany Program" enabled such men to acquire the necessary college courses, including religion and the biblical languages, which equipped them for admission to the Wisconsin Lutheran Seminary. Acknowledging a debt of gratitude to Bethany for twenty-five years of training students for WLS in this way, our synod in 1987 resolved to move the program to Northwestern College where it is now called the Seminary Certification Program.

Unit Eight

HOME MISSION WORK OF OUR CHURCH

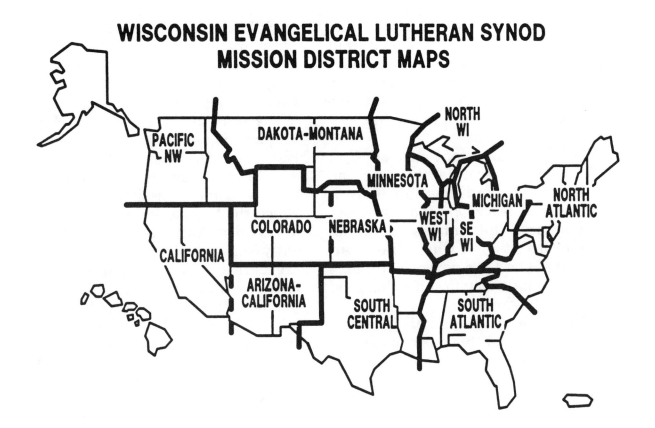

WISCONSIN EVANGELICAL LUTHERAN SYNOD MISSION DISTRICT MAPS

CHAPTER

29. How Home Missions Work

Chapter 29

HOW HOME MISSIONS WORK

"Jesus lives! The victory's won!" That is why we praise our Savior God. And that is why we proclaim him. Often our Lord in his Word points out that he is praised when he is proclaimed. Praising and proclaiming the Lord Jesus is the important mission, or task, which our Lord has graciously given to us.

The most important mission, that of saving sinners, has been accomplished by the Lord himself. The death of our Lord Jesus Christ on the cross has secured the sinner's salvation. The resurrection of Christ has guaranteed it. Our Lord now commissions us and sends us out to share this good news with others.

Jesus clearly informs his followers how to carry out this mission of sharing him and his accomplished mission of saving sinners. In Acts 1:8 Jesus proclaims and promises, "You will receive power when the Holy Spirit comes on you; and you will be my witnesses in Jerusalem, and in all Judea and Samaria, and to the ends of the earth." Under God's grace and guidance, our synod—a group of Christians "walking together" to proclaim and praise our Savior—is still sharing Jesus in similar, ever widening circles today. The first circle is our evangelism effort in our own cities, towns, or counties. The widest circle is work being done through our World Mission Division. The middle circle, encompassing the United States and Canada, involves the Division of Home Missions of our synod.

The work of the Division of Home Missions is under the direction of the Board for Home Missions (BHM), made up of a pastor and lay representative from each of the mission districts into which the United States and Canada are divided. Although our synod presently consists of twelve districts, there are fourteen mission districts. The difference is the result of distance and the number of missions involved.

The Board for Home Missions consists of twenty-eight members and has a chairman who is elected by the synod in convention. The BHM meets to review and evaluate the work of sharing Christ in its circle of responsibility, to adopt policies and procedures which coordinate the work of the various mission districts and to allocate the resources of personnel and money that are available for home mission work.

Each of the fourteen mission districts has a District Mission Board (DMB) which is elected by each district at its conventions. Each district decides how many members to have on its DMB. The DMBs are made up of pastors and laymen who serve on a part-time basis. The members meet regularly to evaluate the work of their circle of responsibility, to provide counsel to missionaries and mission congregations in their district, to decide which steps should be followed next in a mission effort and to determine where the Lord is providing opportunities for sharing him and his gospel with others in their area.

Some DMBs use the services of a mission counselor, a pastor who serves the Lord in the work of home missions on a full-time basis. Not all the fourteen mission districts have their own mission counselor, but some counselors serve more than one mission district. The principal function of the mission counselors is to assist the DMBs in giving counsel to missionar-

ies and mission congregations on suitable ways to reach out with Christ's gospel so that more and more unbelievers will learn of the Lord Jesus and his saving gospel.

To carry out the policies and decisions of the Board for Home Missions and to coordinate the work of the various levels of home mission work, a Home Missions office has been established at the synodical headquarters in Milwaukee, Wisconsin. There, two pastors serve as administrators to coordinate and facilitate the work in the circle of responsibility of Home Missions.

The front edge of the circle of Home Missions is the mission field itself. District Mission Board members, mission counselors, and our fellow Christians inform the District Mission Boards about places where people need to know about Jesus and where our Lord might use us to share him with others. The District Mission Boards select the most

Divine Savior, Pullman, WA

Gethsemane, Kansas City, MO

Redeemer, Rice Lake, WI

St. Luke, Grand Rapids, MN

149

promising mission fields, and the two representatives of each DMB present the God-given opportunities in their areas at the Board for Home Missions meetings. At these meetings the board members prayerfully decide which opportunities to pursue.

Home Missions carries out its mission of sharing God's good news in a variety of ways. At times a group of Christians, together with the DMB, calls a pastor. After the call has been accepted, they assemble for worship in temporary facilities. Unchurched people in the area are invited to join them to hear the good news of their salvation through faith in Christ Jesus.

At other times a mission congregation is formed by calling a pastor to enter a certain area and through hard work gather a congregation. Under God's grace and guidance, the pastor first becomes acquainted with the community and with the people in that community. He does this by knocking on doors, by introducing himself and his mission to the people, and by visiting with them. In whatever way he gets acquainted with people, the missionary always invites them to hear and learn the Scriptures, because they tell about salvation through Christ. As people learn about Jesus and his gospel, the Holy Spirit creates saving faith in some of them and convinces them to want to learn more from Scripture, to worship the Lord and to tell others about him. Then Bible study classes and worship services are begun. Because every believer is a servant of the Lord, believers want to learn ways of telling others about the

Savior. As the believers tell others, the Holy Spirit uses their gospel witnessing to bring some to hear the word, and in time a congregation is born.

Sometimes a congregation or a group of congregations will establish a "daughter" or "foster daughter" congregation and thus widen the circle of believers in Christ in their area. A "daughter" congregation is one in which the parent congregation or congregations provide the money and the ministry to get established. A "foster daughter" congregation is one in which the parent congregation or congregations supply much of the money and the mission boards help direct the work and give counsel to the mission ministry. So that Christ might be shared with as many as possible, the Board for Home Missions likes to remain flexible as to how to plant and grow a mission congregation.

Another responsibility of Home Missions is the Campus Ministry. This ministry recognizes that on college campuses in the United States and Canada many need to learn about Jesus the Savior. Whether through a full-time campus ministry or through a part-time campus ministry of local pastors, efforts are made to gather students to Christ. As the Holy Spirit blesses the spread of the gospel with more believers, those gathered into the church are nurtured with Christ and are taught ways to share the Savior with others on campus.

As a mission congregation grows, it usually seeks help from fellow Christians by borrowing needed money from the synod's Church Extension

Fund. This money is used to purchase a church site, to provide a parsonage for the mission pastor and to construct the worship, education and fellowship facilities. All these are used as a "way station" to which people come to learn that Jesus is the Way, the Truth and the Life. From here new believers go and tell others about Jesus, thus widening the circle still more.

How good and gracious is our Lord God that he uses and blesses our thank offerings to proclaim and praise him! Our thank offerings are used to train pastors and teachers to tell of Jesus and to teach others how to share him with others. Our thank offerings are also used to help support the gospel ministry of mission congregations until they have enough members who are able to support the ministry themselves and the group becomes a self-supporting congregation. Then the mission dollars no longer needed at one place are used somewhere else. Thus the circle widens. Our thank offerings support campus ministry efforts which result in people also serving the Savior where they live after graduating from colleges and universities. Thus our synod's Home Missions carries out its work of enlarging the circle of sharing the Savior.

Unit Nine

WORLD MISSIONS OF OUR CHURCH—PART 1

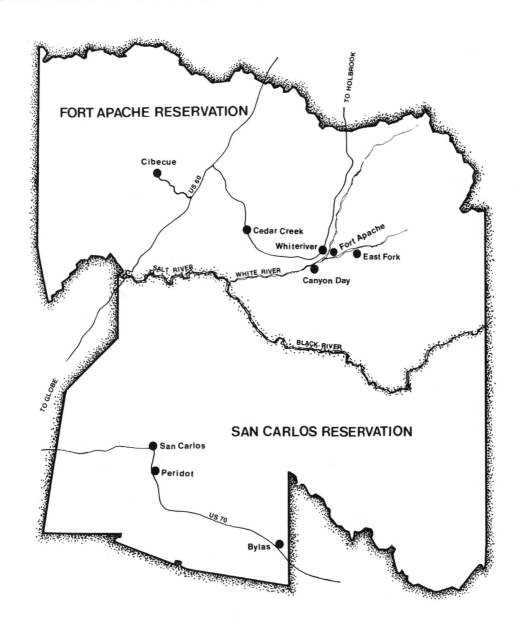

CHAPTERS

Chapter 30

APACHE MISSION

The great work of being witnesses for the gospel to the ends of the earth —in the circle of strangers and friends—is an inspiring story. Begun by the apostles of Christ, especially by St. Paul, this inspiring work is still being carried on and will continue until our Savior returns as the judge of all.

Throughout its history, our Wisconsin Synod has been guided by two statements or commands Jesus made. The first is from the Gospel of St. John: "If you hold to my teaching, you are really my disciples" (8:31); the second is from the book of Acts: "You will be my witnesses . . . to the ends of the earth" (1:8). The remaining chapters of this book will show how our synod carried out the commands of Jesus and continues to carry out the great work of witnessing to the ends of the earth—in the circle of strangers and foreigners.

Search for a Heathen Mission Field

As early as 1883 the synod appointed a committee of five men to find a mission society, either in this country or in Germany, through which it could carry on mission work among the heathen. This committee reported that it could not find a mission society it could recommend.

The synod then decided to look about for young men who would volunteer for future service in heathen mission fields. Three such men began their schooling at Northwestern College in Watertown in the late 1880s. In 1891 the committee reported that within two years these three men, John Plocher, George Adascheck and Paul Mayerhoff, would complete their studies and be ready to go out as missionaries wherever they would be sent.

Having found the men, it was now necessary for our church to select a mission field. In 1892 Pastors O. H. Koch and Theodore Hartwig were sent "into the Southwest to locate a spot where mission work might be started among the Indians." At one time Japan had been considered a likely field, but it was dropped because of the spiritual need in our own Southwest. The two "scouts" were instructed to look for a tribe of Indians among whom no Christian mission work had been done before.

In November 1892 the two pastors began their exploration of the Indian country in Arizona. A Presbyterian missionary among the Pima Indians advised them to go to the San Carlos Reservation of the Apache Indians, assuring them that no mission work had been done among them. What our men heard and saw on their journeys through this country, and what they were told by the government agent, convinced them that they had found in the Apaches exactly the people for whom they had been looking. They reported this when they returned home.

Beautiful Apacheland

The Apache reservation is one of the most beautiful areas of our Southwest. There are actually two reservations: the San Carlos Reservation in the south at an elevation of 2,600 feet above sea level, and the Fort Apache Reservation to the north at an altitude of from 5,000 to 6,000 feet. The southern reservation is largely desert, having a unique beauty of its own, especially when the many cacti and other desert flowers burst into spectacular bloom in spring. The northern reservation has great forests of pine and cedar, spruce and fir, and fast flowing mountain streams and lovely lakes.

The life of the Indians at the time our first missionaries set foot among them was a very difficult one. They had been subdued and confined to cer-

tain areas not entirely of their choosing. Here they had to try to adapt themselves and to eke out their living.

Since the Indians were accustomed to living off the land, housing was no great problem for them. They built their wickiups—as their tents were called—of poles from which the foliage had been stripped. These were stuck, the thicker and heavier ends to the bottom, into the ground in a circle about twelve feet in diameter and tied together with leather or yucca cactus rope at the top. Then it was a simple matter to cover them with thatch made from "bear grass" cactus, blankets or animal hides. Today these wickiups have disappeared and the Indians are living in conventional homes.

Apaches, a Daring Choice

The Apaches whom the first missionaries found on the San Carlos and Fort Apache Reservations were remnants of the most independent and warlike of all the Indian tribes. About 1860 they had gone on the warpath because of cruelties committed against them by a number of white scoundrels. During the Civil War, when the U.S. soldiers were occupied elsewhere, the Apaches drove every white man out of Arizona except a few who found refuge in Tucson. This Indian war raged in Arizona for twenty-five years, and over a thousand men, women and children lost their lives. It was not until 1872 and 1874 that the U.S. Government was able to break up the powerful Indian bands, scattering them into the mountains of Arizona and New Mexico. In 1886 Gen. Nelson A. Miles

forced the ruthless Geronimo and his last band of Apaches to surrender. They were shipped to Florida. The rest of the Apaches were confined to the two reservations. Only seven years after the last bloody battle our first missionaries arrived! The Apaches had by no means forgotten how they had been hunted by armed white soldiers. Their hatred and suspicion of the white man was still very intense.

First Missionaries

Missionaries John Plocher and George Adascheck, recent graduates of our seminary, were sent, not to kill, but to bring the word of peace and life to those who had no hope. In 1893 they began their work in Peridot, in the southern desert.

The work was very difficult and discouraging because, at the beginning, communication between the missionaries and the Apaches was almost impossible. Shortly after the arrival of these two missionaries, Pastor J. F. Gustav Harders joined them. Although he lived in Globe, just off the reservation, he was nevertheless very much interested in the

John Plocher   George Adascheck

156

Apaches. In several novels—*Yaalahn, La Paloma, Dohaschtida*—he revealed his sympathy for the Apaches and described the difficulties encountered by the first missionaries.

Quite understandably, the Apaches at first fiercely resisted the white man. But gradually they not only learned to accept the physical improvements he brought, but many also learned to appreciate salvation in Christ as they came under the influence of the gospel.

Later the Apaches became United States citizens, and today they administer their own affairs. They have also shown loyalty and love to the missionaries who have preached and lived their faith in Christ among them over many years.

For each of the disappointing experiences told by the early missionaries, our pastors and teachers can relate incidents which show the power of the Word of God, replacing hate with love, and hostile behavior with faithful Christian living.

Pastor Harders wrote in 1912: "The Apache is a man who has lost all joy in being alive. He is a man without hope. He walks in darkness and in the shadow of death." How different it is for many of them today!

Chapter 31

APACHE MISSION EXPANDS

Old Cedar at East Fork

During the first years the missionaries at Peridot spent their time in becoming acquainted with the people to whom they had been sent. Gradually they found a few Indians who spoke English well enough to act as interpreters. With these the young missionaries either walked or rode horseback along the trails and dry washes to visit the people in their camps.

While a visit was usually welcomed, it was most difficult to lead the conversation with the Apaches to matters which pertained to the welfare of their souls. Still, the missionaries persisted and, one by one, individuals were won for the gospel of Christ.

It is to the credit of those pioneer missionaries that their activity spread in one year as far north as East Fork on the Fort Apache Reservation. This meant a journey up and over the Nantan Mountains, crossing the Black and White Rivers—when not flooding —into the higher forested regions of the northern reservation. In 1894 Missionaries Plocher and Adascheck reached what is now known as East Fork. Here they pitched their tent under the shade of the oldest tree on the reservation, known today as "Old Cedar." By means of an interpreter

they were able to state the purpose of their coming as messengers of God. It took many sessions to relate the simplest Bible story and to impress the simplest Bible truth on their reluctant hearers.

Inashood

This strange name was given by the Apaches to the missionaries who appeared among them in plain clothing, but on Sundays would function in the simple church services in a long black robe. The Apache, always ready to name a new thing according to its appearance to him, simply called the missionaries *Inashood*, which in Apache means "long gown."

It was the kindly attitude, the helpful hand, the gentle call to repentance and the faith and love of the missionaries which finally broke down the barrier between the white man and the red man. Over the years the goodness of God, shown in Christ our Savior and also in the lives and attitudes of his witnesses, won the hearts of many Apaches, and our missionaries were soon welcomed both on the San Carlos and the Fort Apache reservations. The pioneers who began the mission did not stay long in Apacheland. But as years went by, one mis-

Missionary E. E. Guenther

is taken from the June 7, 1981, issue of the *Northwestern Lutheran*, where it appeared in the "Comments by the Editor" column:

> Mrs. Minnie Guenther, widow of pioneer Missionary E. Edgar Guenther, will be 91 next month. She still lives in Whiteriver, Arizona, and has numerous visitors. —Missionary emeritus Henry Rosin and his wife observed their 60th wedding anniversary in San Carlos last October. —Retired Missionary Alfred Uplegger still does a limited amount of work at San Carlos—64 years after his ordination!

Both Henry Rosin and Alfred Uplegger followed calls into the San Carlos mission immediately after their ordination in 1917. Two years later Dr. Francis Uplegger, his wife, and their daughters followed their son and brother into the mission. One of the Uplegger daughters married Rosin. Dr. Francis labored among the Apaches

sionary after another came to carry the work a little further. Among them were a number of veterans—both men and women—who spent their whole lives on the reservations and literally used themselves up in winning Apaches for Christ.

Veteran Missionaries

One of these was Rev. J. F. Gustav Harders. Another was E. Edgar Guenther, who arrived in Apacheland fresh from the seminary with his young bride in 1911 and was soon adopted formally into the Apache tribe as a blood brother. His long stride and tall stature led the Apaches to call him *Inashood N'daesn*, the Long One. For fifty years he and his wife Minnie were a most welcome sight among the Apaches of the northern reservation.

The following report concerning several pioneer Apache missionaries

Dr. Francis Uplegger

for many decades. He studied the Apache language, which was only a spoken language with no alphabet, by sitting with the Indians in their camps with his notebooks and pictures until he had produced both a vocabulary and a grammar of the Apache language. He then translated much religious material into this difficult tongue.

East Fork Lutheran Nursery

In the early days the Apache Indians regarded babies who were born with deformities as being possessed by evil spirits, and as a result, often left them to die in the desert. Twin babies were treated in the same way. Children of broken homes were left to the mercy of almost anyone who might take an interest in them.

Our missionaries and their wives at first took many of these unfortunate children into their own homes. But it soon became necessary to provide a larger place to care for such children, so Missionary and Mrs. E. E. Guenther started an orphanage at East Fork.

At first there were no funds. For years cartons and boxes had to serve as baby cribs and bassinets. Finally in 1957, the East Fork Nursery and Child Placing Agency was created in order to find Apache Christian homes for abandoned children. This work is supported by individuals and by the ladies' organizations of our Wisconsin Synod.

Outstanding among the women who have served in this work of caring for those whom Jesus called "the greatest

East Fork Nursery

in the kingdom of heaven" is Miss Louise Kutz. For many years this Christian lady dedicated her life to the happiness and eternal welfare of unfortunate Apache children. A dormitory for the nurses and attendants has been named in her honor.

Apache Schools

One of the best means to approach the Apaches is through their children. From the beginning, Christian school classes were arranged for the little ones. In this way our Lutheran elementary schools came into being in Apacheland. That they are a blessing is apparent, for our congregations today largely consist of those who have enjoyed a Christian education in our four Apache Lutheran elementary schools.

This phase of mission work was expanded when the East Fork Academy, now the East Fork Lutheran High School, was founded in 1948. This is a boarding school on the East Fork Mission compound, where students of high school age are given an opportunity for a secondary education under

Christian influence. One of the men who was most active in this work was Teacher Arthur Meier, who devoted over thirty years to the Christian education of young Apaches. A long-awaited new girls' dormitory was completed and dedicated in the spring of 1981. The Apache congregations at San Carlos and Peridot collected $6,000 as their special contribution for this excellently equipped building.

In those congregations where we have no day schools, as at San Carlos and Whiteriver, very active and efficient Sunday schools, vacation Bible schools, Junior Bible classes, Lutheran Pioneers and Luther League bring the gospel to Indian children of all ages, as do Bible classes to Indian parents.

Does It Pay?

For years the missionaries have had to answer the oft-repeated questions, "Does it pay?" "Are we making any progress?" Actually, these questions could be asked of any missionary activity, because our Wisconsin Synod does not have a history of im-

Cedar Creek Church

pressive numerical gains in missions.

When one considers the difficulties which had to be overcome in Apacheland—the loss of freedom for a nomadic people, the confinement to a reservation and the difficulty of getting a livelihood—one can well imagine that the mission program was slow. One must also remember that at first our missionaries did not learn Apache. They preached and taught only through interpreters and gathered freedom-loving nomadic people into confining churches and schools. Still, we can also record wonderful triumphs for the preaching of the gospel in the earlier times of the mission. In recent years missionaries have also had to adapt to changes in Indian life styles.

The Apaches became wards of the government in 1886. They engaged in industries such as cattle raising, logging and farming. But in recent years many of the better educated moved off the reservations and found employment elsewhere. They frequently became members of our churches in their new localities. Unemployment among the Apaches creates additional problems.

The life of the Apache family has changed greatly. Apaches no longer live in wickiups. Frame houses, housing developments and new buildings are springing up in many areas. The modern pick-up and family car have almost replaced the horse, except for round-ups. Shops, super-markets, restaurants and theaters are crowding out the colorful old trading posts.

161

Spiritual Changes

Changes just as great as those experienced by the Apaches in their occupations and way of life have also taken place in their churches. In 1981 Lutheran Apaches numbered about 3,000, out of a total population of nearly 16,000 on both reservations. Many of them have had the benefit of religious training from parents—and some from grandparents—who attended the Lutheran elementary schools and the East Fork Lutheran High School.

The changes are apparent in many ways. Apache church members are becoming more and more active in church life. They attend services more regularly and partake of the Lord's Supper more often. Their officers and councils administer the churches on the reservations. Apache laymen attend the Arizona-California District and the synod conventions as delegates.

The Apache Lutherans demonstrated their zeal for the work of their Savior after the building which housed the East Fork Lutheran High School was destroyed by fire in November 1986. Up to this time the Apache Lutherans were not involved as leaders in the affairs of the high school. Instead, the school was operated by the faculty under the direction of the Apache Mission Executive Committee of the Board for World Missions. But as a result of the destructive explosion

The new East Fork Lutheran Schools

and fire, the Apaches not only influenced the construction of a new building but also formed a local board which controls the affairs of the East Fork Lutheran High School.

Their growing willingness to help themselves is evident both in their increased offerings and in the work projects which have been carried out by them in almost every parish. The members at Whiteriver have built an educational unit largely with their own means and muscle. At Peridot the members built a new teacherage, borrowing the money for the material and contributing their own labor. At East Fork they built much of the addition to their new church. Contributions of Apache Lutherans for their synod's work give evidence of their interest in the church-at-large. Their offerings are sent in regularly for World Mission fields in Japan, Taiwan and other places.

The fire at East Fork Lutheran School

Unit Ten

WORLD MISSIONS OF OUR CHURCH—PART 2

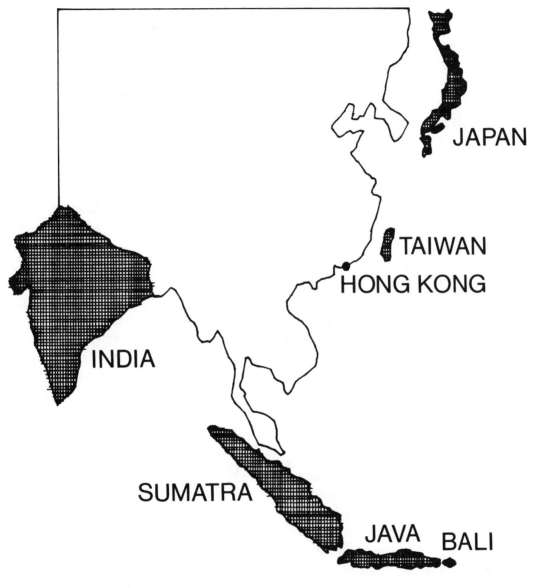

JAPAN

TAIWAN

HONG KONG

INDIA

SUMATRA

JAVA

BALI

CHAPTERS

Chapter 32

JAPAN, OUR FIRST ASIAN MISSION

Beginnings

In its first hundred years, our church did not experience the joy of opening a mission of its own in a foreign land. It carried on missions among Apaches, Lutherans in Poland and Spanish-speaking people in Tucson. Our church did participate in mission work in Nigeria, but that work was conducted jointly with the other synods of the Synodical Conference.

In 1951 our church was faced with two requests—to open a new mission in Africa and one in Japan. With a firm faith in God's promises, the delegates voted to enter both fields.

Our first missionary to Japan was Rev. Fred G. Tiefel. He was sent to Tokyo to serve the U.S. military personnel of our synod, and he was asked to explore the possibilities of establishing a mission among the Japanese. Because of their recent defeat in World War II, the Japanese were very reluctant to have anything to do with Americans and Christian missionaries. This made Pastor Tiefel's assignment extra difficult.

Pastor Tiefel immediately set about learning the Japanese language and translating certain writings, such as Luther's Small Catechism, into that language. During the course of five years he instructed a number of young Japanese who formed a small congregation. In 1957, however, our church lost this mission when Pastor Tiefel left our fellowship. The Board for World Missions then made a fresh start and first called Pastor Richard Seeger and shortly thereafter Pastor Richard Poetter to serve in Japan.

Language Difficulties

There are many cultural shocks experienced by a missionary who goes to a foreign country. In a country like Japan he will face great language difficulties. Probably the greatest problem is that many thoughts and expressions related to our Christian religion, such as "sin," "grace" and "Trinity," are entirely unknown there. Besides, many words, like "love" and "forgiveness," may have an entirely different meaning in a foreign culture. This makes it necessary for the missionary to learn exactly how to express a Bible truth in the language of the people so that they correctly understand gospel truths. The missionary must, for example, be very careful not simply to take over their name for God, assuming that they will understand him to mean the God of the Holy Bible rather than some family or national god. It requires an entire year for a missionary to learn to speak Japanese, and many more years to learn to express himself clearly and unmistakably in matters of religion. It is indeed an accomplishment when a missionary can preach his first sermon in Japanese.

Fear of Persecution

Mission work in Japan is slow and difficult for another reason. Any Japanese who goes to a Christian missionary for instruction or to the Christian chapel for worship may lose his friends, be disowned by his family or be dismissed from his job. It takes the kind of courage shown by a nineteen-year-old Japanese girl. One of our missionaries reported that on the night before her baptism, she called and said, "My father won't let me be baptized. What should I do?" The missionary encouraged her to pray about it and said he would also pray. The next morning as the service began the young lady was not present. During the singing of the baptismal hymn however, there was a small commotion. The missionary looked up and saw the young lady walking down the aisle. Everyone in the room clapped spontaneously, hard and long. The missionary wrote: "How the angels must have rejoiced at that spontaneous burst of praise!" A week later he asked her, "What did your father say when you were baptized?" "I didn't tell him. He didn't ask," she said.

Vast Field

Japan has more than 120 million inhabitants, the vast majority being Shintoists and Buddhists. Many are disillusioned with these religions, but it is very difficult to reach them with the Christian message. For a missionary, whether American or Japanese, to go to a person's home to speak to him about his soul's welfare is considered an intrusion of one's privacy.

The only access the Christian missionary has into the home is through the radio or the printed word. Radio is expensive, but our two fifteen-minute broadcasts twice each Sunday continue to bring in contacts each week. The mission print shop also produces much needed material to carry out Jesus' Great Commission. The material includes Sunday school lessons, the Japanese Lutheran Church paper, catechism correspondence, Bible camp circulars and newspaper "slip-ins." Many prospects are gained by these means, but it will be a long time before the church can reach even a tiny fraction of the millions living in Japan.

Japanese are very intelligent and ambitious. In their high schools, English is a required study. This proved to be an opening wedge at Utsonomiya, where the missionary was approached by groups of businessmen and leading townspeople with the request to teach them English. He suggested that they come together once a week to read one of the finest pieces of English literature—the Holy Bible. So a Bible class came into being. It resulted in the conversion of several prominent people in that community.

Missionary Work Force

Our church has had as many as seven missionaries in Japan from the

United States, and one teacher, who instructs our missionaries' children. There are four fully-trained Japanese pastors working full time in the large prefectures, or states, north of Tokyo. Churches have been built, and a seminary has been operating since 1967 at Tsuchiura. Missionaries at Tsuchiura and from nearby congregations assist as instructors.

The synod's Japanese mission program began at Tokyo. Our new missionaries find it easier to learn the language in this large city because of its many schools. Tokyo also serves as a hub of our mission work in Japan. Most of the highways and railroads fan out from the city and are usually in much better condition than the roads which tie the cities and towns of outlying areas together. Japan's excellent railway system makes it possible for members and prospects to reach one or the other of our strategically located churches in the Tokyo area without difficulty.

Building the Japanese Church

The beginnings in a foreign mission are usually very small and very slow. Pastor Poetter spent more than a year before he baptized his first two converts at Mito on November 29, 1959. Yet, though there were only two, it was a start.

Some people think of foreign missions as a "give-away" program in which the home churches donate all the money and the laborers and the new converts are never expected to do anything for themselves. The very opposite is the case. It is true that we

Mito Church, Japan

support the missionaries who go in our place to a people who do not know the Savior. But from the very beginning our missionaries teach the converts to share the Good News about their Savior with neighbors and friends, to find people in their own groups willing to be trained as pastors and teachers and to provide the necessary funds or materials to construct whatever buildings are needed.

The Lutheran Evangelical Christian Church of Japan (LECC) has its own Church Extension Fund, which was begun with over $20,000 in gifts collected from groups and individuals in our U.S. congregations. In 1980, $25,000 borrowed from this fund plus $150,000 from the World Mission Building Fund and a gift of $25,000 from a dedicated Christian family made possible the purchase of land, chapel and parsonage in Chiba City, a rapidly growing suburb of Tokyo located near the new Narita airport. The CEF loans are, of course, repaid by the Japanese congregations so that other churches may borrow from the fund.

"Bamboo"

"Narcissus

"Plum Blossoms"

"Pine"

Sumi-e Art by IKU, a member of the LECC in Japan

167

Deacon Ryuichi (ree-yu-EE-chee) Igarashi deserves a special word of praise. An educated Japanese, who also speaks Russian, German and English, he joined Rev. Richard Poetter's congregation more than twenty-five years ago and helped him to learn and use the best style of Japanese in his sermons and writings. Now holding the honorary office of deacon, Igarashi Sensei (sen-SAY, meaning

Deacon Igarashi second from left

"the Honorable") has served Superintendent Poetter and placed his great gifts in the service of his Savior to reach all Japanese with the gospel in the language and style his countrymen expect of teachers and leaders.

He not only translates various materials and pamphlets and publishes them in Japanese but takes care of legal matters pertaining to real estate and taxes.

First Love

The congregations in Japan are much more closely-knit than ours in the United States. They consist of people who were won for Christ by someone in the same church. As a result, there is within the congregations a happy spirit of fellowship and concern which expresses itself in shared Bible study and hymn singing and in frequent, friendly get-togethers. It is not uncommon for a whole congregation to hire a bus to go as a group to a dedication, the installation of a pastor or to a summer Bible camp. Christmas especially is a joyous occasion in the Japanese church. This happy sense of belonging together and of working together reminds one of the first love in the early Christian church, as it is described in the last verses of the second chapter of Acts.

Chapter 33

SOUTHEAST ASIAN MISSIONS

Hong Kong

In 1970 the Chinese Evangelical Lutheran Church (CELC), an independent church body affiliated with our church, seemed to be the most promising and fastest growing of all our missions. There was an almost storybook quality about its beginnings. In 1950 a Lutheran deaconess pressed a penny Bible tract into the hands of a young Chinese whose wealthy family had lost most of its property when the Communists came into power in China. The family had fled to the British island colony of Hong Kong.

After reading the tract, the young man decided to give up his plans of becoming a businessman and to devote his life to sharing with his fellow Chinese his joy in finding the Savior. Within ten years he gathered three congregations in a confessional church. He then came to America, studied for the Lutheran ministry at Mankato, Minnesota, and, after passing his examinations, was ordained. In the meanwhile he had appealed to our synod for fellowship, and the synod sent a number of "friendly counselors," one after the other, to Hong Kong to direct the work of winning souls for Christ and to instruct Chi-

nese nationals in a seminary founded at the time.

Soon the CELC was operating three schools on the rooftops of large apartment buildings. The Chinese pastor gave them names that reflected the subjects taught: "Spirit of Love," "Spirit of Grace," and "Immanuel." He developed a radio program, "The Voice of Salvation," and beamed it northward into Communist China, where all Christian missionaries were banned, and eastward to the island of Taiwan, where Nationalist Chinese were in control.

A spirit of optimism prevailed in our church, but it was soon learned that it may have been a case of too much too soon or of the seed falling upon shallow soil that could not sustain the plants that sprang up quickly and then withered. At any rate, the Chinese leader who had been instrumental in bringing our church to Hong Kong left both the ministry and the colony and became a businessman in America. The schools and the seminary closed, and the remaining handful of Chinese nationals petitioned the court for the dissolution of the "independent" CELC via bankruptcy.

Rising phoenix-like from ashes, the Southeast Asia Lutheran Evangelical

Mission (SALEM) appeared. It was a humbler but more solidly based organization, recognized by the Hong Kong government and supervised by personnel from our church. This is now our Hong Kong Mission.

SALEM was a complete reorganization of our mission in Hong Kong. The missionaries of this reorganized church labor to train as many Chinese as possible in understanding Scripture and to equip many full-time workers. The five-man mission team (four pastors and one teacher) has established several effective ways to reach and teach the young Chinese. These are the Immanuel Lutheran Study Centre, the Immanuel Lutheran College, a Bible institute and a seminary.

There is a certain urgency in reaching and teaching as many Chinese with God's Word as possible and in preparing them to carry on the mission work in Hong Kong without the guidance and assistance of American missionaries. The British, who presently control Hong Kong, have agreed to relinquish their authority over this

Lai King Lutheran Study, Center, Hong Kong

dependency and to place it under the control of the People's Republic of China (Communist China). This transfer of authority is scheduled to occur in 1997. It could happen that the Chinese Communists will prohibit our American missionaries from proclaiming the gospel of salvation in Hong Kong after 1997, so we prepare for that time and leave the outcome in the Lord's hands.

Taiwan

The churches in Taiwan are living proof that God's revealed message does not return to him empty. (Isaiah 55:11) As a result of the "Voice of Salvation" radio broadcasts and a visit by one of our friendly counselors and the Chinese leader from Hong Kong, three congregations were formed on the island—two in the capital city of Taipei and one in Everlasting Happiness Village. Today the aim of our missionaries in Taiwan is to forge strong ties and working relationships with these national churches and their evangelists, two of whom received their training in the short-lived Hong Kong seminary.

Grace Church—Seminary, Missionary Apartments, Hong Kong

Church in Everlasting Happiness Village

Many heathen live in this island nation of close to twenty million people. The vast majority of these people are literate, but many of them believe in ancestor worship or Buddhism or Taoism. To give the heathen Taiwanese, who live in spiritual darkness, the light of the gospel, our church supports four missionaries, who together with a national pastor and other workers, aggressively proclaim God's Word in the Chinese Mandarin language.

Indonesia

Indonesia, a country consisting of more than 13,500 islands, lies between the southeastern part of mainland Asia and the continent of Australia. Approximately 160 million people inhabit Indonesia, with about three-fifths of those people living on the island of Java. Like Taiwan, Indonesia is predominantly heathen, for about 90% of the Indonesians are Muslims, while only 5% belong to various Christian denominations. From this heathen country our church received a "call" to begin mission work.

There was no direct connection between the church at Hong Kong and the "call" from Indonesia as there was in the case of Taiwan. Yet the mission in Indonesia began among Chinese-speaking Indonesians, and here, as in Hong Kong, our church was brought into the picture by another young Chinese pastor. He had studied to become a missionary of another church body but was later converted to Lutheranism by reading a book on Lutheran doctrine.

At his request members of our Board for World Missions made two visits to Indonesia to discuss matters with him and survey the prospects for opening a new mission. Though this young pastor later severed the fellowship that had been declared between him and our church, the small group of Christians was saved for us by a loyal evangelist, J. E. Epiphanius. To this day the now aged Epiphanius works with our synod's missionary in the city of Sukabumi.

Congregation in Sukabumi, Indonesia

Equally loyal and effective assistance is given our missionaries in Jakarta, the Indonesian capital, by Rev. Anak Agung Dipa Pandji Tisna. The son of an ex-king of Bali, Pandji Tisna came to know Christ by attending the

171

Lutheran services in Sukabumi. After being instructed, baptized and confirmed, he received his theological training in the Hong Kong seminary. For the last few years he has been working in close harmony with our three missionaries in the outlying areas of Jakarta, where no Christian missions are presently located. An English-speaking congregation and a smaller Indonesian group meet regularly for worship. Both Sukabumi and Jakarta are situated on the island of Java.

Problems and Prospects

Being understaffed and experiencing difficulties in getting visas for American pastors to carry on Christian mission activities in a Moslem-dominated country are among the problems experienced in our Southeast Asian missions. Yet the problems and difficulties of mission work in this distant part of the world are as nothing compared to the glorious promises of Scripture, first spoken for the comfort of Israel, but also meant for all New Testament believers: "Enlarge the place of your tent, stretch your tent curtains wide, do not hold back; lengthen your cords, strengthen your stakes" (Isaiah 54:2). Words like these inspire the faith of missionaries and of those who send them. Each year, for example, the Board for World Missions receives testimonials of faith from members in the form of special gifts. They range from the five dollars saved by a schoolboy to the gift of $65,000 from a single family, asking that it be used to provide chapels in our world mission fields. The Southeast Asian committee, trusting in the word of the Lord that "the islands will look to me and wait in hope for my arm" (Isaiah 51:5), is ready with plans to call more pastors and teachers to each of the island missions to enlarge and "strengthen their stakes."

India

In reports concerning the mission in India the words "no," "none," and "nothing" recur with depressing regularity from biennium to biennium. There is no change in government policy: No foreign missionaries are allowed to enter the country. The number of children or adults either baptized or confirmed is "none," and there is nothing by way of change or favorable outlook.

Yet the story of the origin of this mission seemed to be as full of promise as it was fascinating. The wife of one of our pastors wrote her name on the flyleaf of a Bible being sent to India. To her great surprise she received a letter from a Mr. T. Paul Mitra, who inquired about the Lutheran church. The inquiry was brought to the attention of the Board for World Missions. One thing led to another. We learned that Mr. T. Paul Mitra (a university graduate), his wife (a registered medical doctor) and his two sisters (registered school teachers) were carrying on a Lutheran mission entirely without outside help among the forgotten farmers and villagers on the eastern seacoast near Madras. The work originally was begun by Mr. Mitra's father.

Since India closed its doors to foreign missionaries, the Board for World Missions arranged to have Mr. Mitra and his wife come to the United States to audit courses in theology at our seminary. In this way Paul Mitra was able to fulfill his life's wish to become an ordained Lutheran pastor. The synod built a modest chapel-dispensary for him in India as a center from which to continue his work under our guidance and supervision. Individuals and societies also raised money to purchase a van for him and his wife.

But the Mitras are growing old. The prayer now is that a new leader may emerge to take the place of this dedicated pair and strengthen the stakes of the tiny Lutheran flock in a strange and distant land.

Chapter 34

CENTRAL ASIA RADIO COMMITTEE

In the late 1700s Catherine the Great, empress of Russia, convinced more than 7,000 German families to emigrate to Russia and settle along the Volga River and in the region north of the Black Sea. Over 75% of these Germans were of the Lutheran faith. After more than ten years of great difficulties in battling the wilderness and defending themselves against marauding robber bands and fierce Mongolian nomads, these Germans experienced over 100 years of relative peace.

But this changed. Beginning in 1936 the Russian Germans suffered persecution from the Soviet communist government. The Soviet leader, Joseph Stalin, had the vast majority of the Germans shipped to labor camps in Siberia and central Asia. It is estimated that nearly 2,000,000 displaced Germans are scattered throughout the cities and rural communities of Siberia, Kazakstan and other central Asian provinces.

Living under the domination of Soviet atheism, the German Lutherans are denied freedom of worship. To provide these scattered German Lutherans with the gospel, our church, at its 1983 convention, voted to establish the Central Asia Radio Committee. This committee was commissioned to develop a German-language radio broadcast, which would use the airwaves to proclaim God's Word throughout central Asia.

The Central Asia Radio Committee developed a weekly half-hour worship service and gave it the title *Dies ist der Tag* from the opening words of Psalm 118:24, "This is the day. . . . " These half-hour German worship services are broadcast from two shortwave stations, one in South Korea and the other on the western Pacific island of Saipan, which lies about 1,600 miles southeast of Tokyo.

The first *Dies ist der Tag* broadcast occurred on Epiphany Sunday, January 6, 1985. The non-budgetary Central Asia Radio Fund provides the money to pay for the cost of these gospel-proclaiming German broadcasts. Professor Daniel Deutschlander of Northwestern College prepares and records the services.

Unit Eleven

WORLD MISSIONS OF OUR CHURCH—PART 3

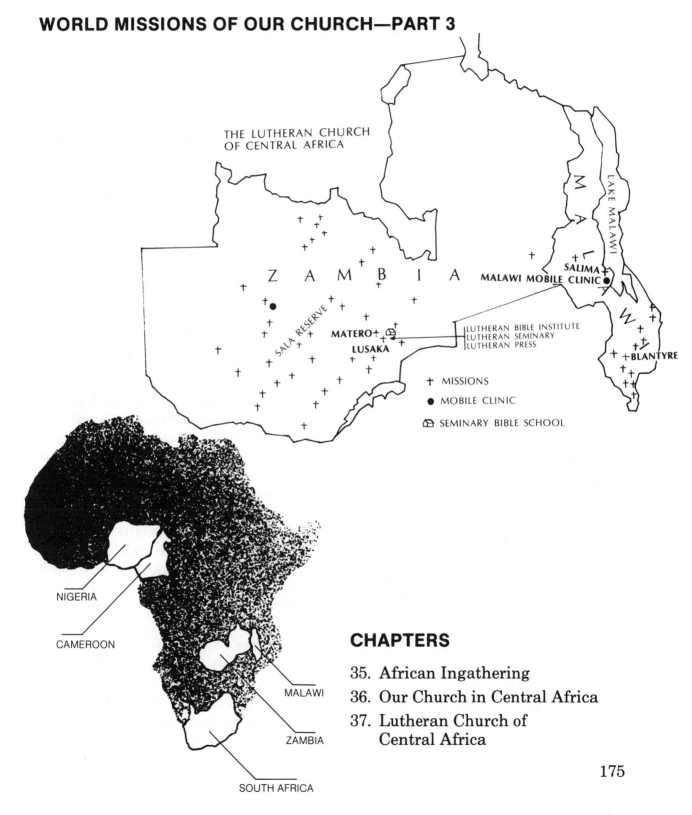

THE LUTHERAN CHURCH OF CENTRAL AFRICA

ZAMBIA

SALA RESERVE

MATERO
LUSAKA

LUTHERAN BIBLE INSTITUTE
LUTHERAN SEMINARY
LUTHERAN PRESS

MALAWI MOBILE CLINIC
SALIMA

LAKE MALAWI

MALAWI

BLANTYRE

✝ MISSIONS
● MOBILE CLINIC
⌂ SEMINARY BIBLE SCHOOL

NIGERIA
CAMEROON
MALAWI
ZAMBIA
SOUTH AFRICA

CHAPTERS

175

Chapter 35

AFRICAN INGATHERING

African Missions in Bible Times

Of all our world mission fields, Africa is the fastest growing. In a single year Malawi membership increased by thirty-one percent, children's confirmations by 476 percent and adult confirmations by sixty-one percent. One of the missionaries in that country wrote: "Our concern is that we can't cope with the harvest and maintain our existing churches properly. A joyous problem we haven't faced anywhere before, I think."

The African ingathering was foretold in Psalm 68:31: "Envoys will come from Egypt; Cush [the southern Nile region] will submit herself to God." The actual missionary work in Africa began in the apostlic age when Philip the Evangelist was sent by the Holy Spirit to instruct and baptize a high official of the court of Candace, the queen of Ethiopia. When this man had been instructed by Philip and confessed, "I believe that Jesus Christ is the Son of God," Philip baptized him. The man went on his way rejoicing in his Savior. Surely, he shared his joy with his people in Ethiopia when he came home.

Simon, the man who was forced to carry Jesus' cross on the way to Calvary, was from Cyrene, the country west of Egypt on the Mediterranean Sea. Simon's wife and their son Rufus are mentioned by St. Paul as people "chosen in the Lord" (Romans 16:13). On the great day of Pentecost there were people from Egypt, Libya and Cyrene who heard St. Peter's sermon and became believers in Christ. "Men from Cyprus and Cyrene . . . began to speak to Greeks also, telling them the good news about the Lord Jesus" (Acts 11:20).

In 1872 our Wisconsin Synod joined with the Missouri Synod to form the Synodical Conference of North America. Five years later this federation of confessional churches resolved to give expression to their unity of faith and confession by opening joint mission work among the black people of our country, especially in the deep South. For a long time the main work was carried on in the rural sections of Alabama. When many black people moved into larger cities, the missions followed them. Our own synod today has such city missions in Detroit, Milwaukee and Minneapolis.

Two schools were founded for training black pastors and teachers. The one at Greensboro, North Carolina, survived as a combined academy, college and seminary.

Miss Rosa J. Young was the instrument in God's hands that brought our Lutheran church to Alabama and with it the blessing of the precious gospel for the black people of the South. The man who pioneered the work among the southern blacks was Pastor N. J. Bakke, who confirmed the first class of converts in 1916.

Africa Calls

The African Mission of the Synodical Conference began in 1936 when the first missionary, Dr. Henry Nau, arrived in Nigeria. He had been sent in response to a letter which was received in 1930 from Mr. J. E. Eka as an appeal of the Ibesikpo Clan of southern Nigeria. This is, in part, what he wrote:

I, on behalf of all the 40 towns of Ibesikpo in Calabar Province of South Nigeria have the honor to approach the President or General Superintendent and all the members of your famous Lutheran Mission per you for the first time on an important point which requires an immediate and urgent attention from you.

It was only last week that we had a letter from that youngster of ours telling us to apply to you to come over to our "Macedonia" to help us, else we die.

We earnestly, sincerely and humbly ask you to our town of Ibesikpo and establish the proposed Negro Mission here, thus making Ibesikpo the headquarters, and all the surrounding towns and countries will flock in for the same request.

The "youngster" mentioned in the letter refers to Mr. Jonathan E. Ekong, whom the Ibesikpo people had sent to America to study for the ministry. While attending several Negro colleges in the South, he was led to our Lutheran mission. Here he was instructed and confirmed, attended the Lutheran Seminary, returned to his people in Africa, and for years served as pastor of a large congregation at Obot Idim and as President of the Lutheran Church of Nigeria.

The Cry for Help Is Heeded

In the letter from Nigeria, reference is made to "the proposed Negro Mission here." Actually, the black churches of the Synodical Conference had long been gathering money for some kind of mission work in Africa. With this money a committee was sent to Nigeria to investigate the call for help. As a result of their very favorable report, the Synodical Conference decided in 1935 to take up mission work in Nigeria.

Dr. Henry Nau, the first missionary to be sent to Nigeria, reported at the

end of his one year's service in the field, "We found sixteen congregations when we came (April 1936). We left thirty-two in the hands of our successors. We started in the midst of one clan. We were working among six clans when we left."

Pastor William Schweppe of our synod, then only twenty-nine years of age, took over the work from Dr. Nau in 1937 and carried on as missionary

Missionary William Schweppe, on the left

178

and superintendent until he accepted the call to our synod's mission in Central Africa in 1960.

During Pastor Schweppe's twenty-three years of faithful service, the mission developed into the Evangelical Lutheran Church of Nigeria. Before the Nigerian civil war in 1969 this church had a membership of 35,000, an enrollment of 16,310 children in 86 Christian day schools, 239 in the high school, 55 in preparatory training schools, 105 in the teachers' college and 44 in the seminary. The church was served by 19 American missionaries, 17 African pastors, 3 American teachers, 8 American medical missionaries, 3 American lay missionaries, and 593 African Lutheran teachers.

Our church played a very important part in this development. Under Pastor William Schweppe the work expanded into the Ogoja Province and Ghana, a large modern hospital was built with the gift of one of our laymen, and the theological seminary at Obot Idim, under the able direction of Professor Norbert Reim, developed a corps of confessionally sound Lutheran pastors.

Christ the King Lutheran Synod

This participation in the Nigerian work was terminated in 1963, when our synod withdrew from the Synodical Conference. By this time our mission in Central Africa had completed its first decade, and Pastor Schweppe and our other Nigerian missionaries were called to serve in Zambia.

Then, in the late 1960s, congregations in the Abak area of southeastern

Nigeria left the Nigerian Lutheran Church for confessional reasons and formed Christ the King Lutheran Synod. They appealed to our church for help in July 1969. The pastor of the congregations, Rev. E. U. Eshiett, came to America and attended our Wisconsin Lutheran Seminary from January to May of 1974.

At first we supplied a subsidy through Aid to Sister Synods Fund. Later, in 1977, a special Aid for Nigeria Fund was created. One of the principal needs of this African synod was an educational program to strengthen its ministry. Presently our mission board arranges seminars twice a year for the workers and lay leaders in Nigeria. They are conducted by qualified instructors from our church. The 1,000 souls of Christ the King Synod are being served by three national pastors and other trained church workers.

Chapter 36

OUR CHURCH IN CENTRAL AFRICA

Africa Is Chosen

August of 1945 was a memorable month. Gratitude toward the Lord had been the keynote of the 1945 synodical convention, because 1945 marked the successful conclusion of a ten-year effort by members of the synod to pay off the huge debt which for years had hampered every department of our church in its work and progress. Finally, the pledge which had been made ten years earlier, that the synod would move forward in home and world missions if the debt was removed, could be fulfilled.

And so the delegates of the 1945 convention instructed the Board for World Missions to explore new mission fields, especially in Africa. Our board knew very little about Africa, its mission opportunities and its problems. It resolved, therefore, to send a team of two pastors to explore the African continent for a promising mission site. Three and a half years later two pastors, Edgar Hoenecke and Arthur Wacker, were persuaded to undertake the survey.

African Mission Safari

The first four months of 1949 were a nightmare of feverish preparation for the long trek. Since the route of travel

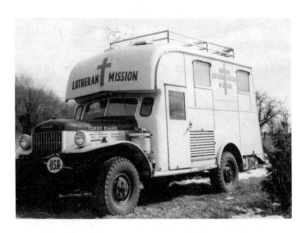

"Caravan", the house on wheels

was to be through remote areas of Africa, not covered by other missions, a vehicle had to be outfitted with living quarters and supplies for six months. A one-ton Dodge Power Wagon chassis was bought and a heavy steel body and cab were built on it. This ungainly vehicle, painted white with a golden cross and the legend "Lutheran African Mission—Exploratory Expedition" in black letters, was equipped with double-decker cots, an auxiliary power generator, a butanegas stove, table and chairs, storage lockers, fuel and water tanks, and enough food and provisions for six months. Assembling all the necessary gear was another staggering task! Finally, in the gray dawn of the second Monday after Easter, the huge vehicle rolled out of the driveway at Plymouth, Michigan, and headed down the turnpike for Brooklyn. Twenty-one days later the freighter *African Crescent* desposited truck and explorers at Capetown on the southern tip of Africa. The 7,500 mile trek through Africa was about to begin.

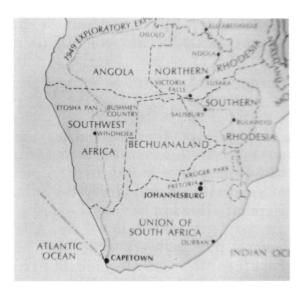

1949 exploration

Mission Field Discovery

Beginning at Capetown, the mission safari proceeded northward through the fruitful Paarl District. They crossed the Orange River on a very shaky wooden ferry, propelled by long poles in the hands of sturdy African men who spoke Dutch and German besides their own vernacular. From here the journey went on and on through the desert on very rough roads to Windhoek, the capital of Namibia (Southwest Africa). Here it took over a week to have the broken springs and brakes repaired.

The road now led through the Etosha Pan, a large, dry lake bed, abounding in game of all kinds. It is also the home of the tribe of Bushmen who entertained the missionaries with their singing around the evening camp fire. One of the songs they sang, and that in a high falsetto voice, was "A Mighty Fortress Is Our God."

From Ovamboland north the road became a mere trail of two wheel tracks or spoors, as the Dutch Afrikaaners call them. These also disappeared, and there was nothing left to do but to break a trail through the tall elephant grass across the veld (pronounced "feld" and means "field"). Often at night it looked as though all Africa was afire. The Africans regularly burn off the grass to prevent spontaneous fires from consuming their grass and thatch huts and to clear the land for the next crop.

Crossing the Kunene, the second river in over a thousand miles of coastline, the missionaries found themselves in Portuguese Angola, a lush, sub-tropical country. However, it was not until they crossed to the other side of Africa, after driving through Angola and southern Zaire (Belgian Congo), that the missionaries finally found a promising, virgin mission field in what was then known as Northern Rhodesia, but is now called Zambia.

Prayer Under the Big Baobab Tree

The area suggested to the road-weary travelers by several missionaries whom they had visited on the long eastward trek through the forest and jungle was known as "the Hook of the

Kafue Native Development Center," west of Lusaka, the capital of Zambia.

As the two Wisconsin Synod explorers settled down for the first night at Lusaka on July 6, 1949, they spoke a heartfelt prayer of thanksgiving to the Lord for having led them after four months to an ideal mission site. The far-spreading branches of the mighty baobab tree under which they parked that night beside the Government Administration Building seemed symbolic of their prayers and of the Lord's sheltering arms.

Here, finally, they had found a haven of rest and hope after their long quest of almost three months. Now, under a friendly government, Christian officials in a land where English was spoken—in a promising, virgin field—a mission could flourish. Ours would be the first Lutheran church in this large, undeveloped land.

Mission Beginning— Four Years Later

The Hook of the Kafue area, however, was no longer open to our synod when our first missionaries arrived four years later. Administrator Sir John Moffatt had waited for us, but after two years had to open the field to another mission agency. Nine calls had been placed by our Mission Board before Pastor A. B. Habben accepted. A second man, Candidate Otto Drevlow, a graduate of Bethany Seminary at Mankato, Minnesota, was assigned to the African mission after completion of his studies. Mr. Paul Ziegler was engaged to assist the missionaries in erecting the necessary buildings.

At first the families lived in mobile homes or trailers, which they brought with them to Africa. Pastor Habben and Mr. Ziegler arrived at Lusaka on June 19, 1953; on June 28 the first service was held with a group of Europeans. Although the mission from the beginning was planned to bring the gospel to the African people, the request of these Lutheran people could not be denied. This congregation, composed of people of various racial backgrounds, continues to this day.

Work Expands

In September the missionaries went out to the Sala Reserve and met with Chief Shakumbila and the headmen of several Sala villages. The Salas were interested in having the Lutheran pastors work among them. After several meetings, the chief and his headmen offered to set aside 160 acres of high ground under the Twin Palms at Lumano for the Lutheran Mission.

This offer was accepted and, with the permission of the Sala tribe, the missionaries moved their house trailers under the Twin Palms. After visiting most of the villages in the Sala Reserve, acquainting the people with the gospel of Christ and inviting them to be instructed, the missionaries held the first service at Lumano on April 11, 1954. The first to be baptized were Headman Symonde and old Jack Mwachele. During the same year the first unit of the Martin Luther Boarding School was built at Lumano, and services and instruction classes were begun in fifteen other village schools on the Sala Reserve. In the meantime work had also begun among the Africans in the Matero African suburb of Lusaka. This mission grew very rapidly.

The work was expanded quickly on the Sala Reserve when the missionaries were invited to hold classes and services in the village schools and were given the management of these schools by the Department of Education. However, because this became too time-consuming and the mission had to accept teachers in the schools who were not Christians and whose principles and behavior violated scriptural teaching and practice, the school management was given up in 1965. This did not affect the privilege of holding classes and Lutheran services in these schools.

The Land

Zambia and Malawi are about as far south of the Equator as Nigeria is north of it, but they are much higher in elevation. This central African region, about 4,000 feet above sea level, is known as "tropical savannah land." Zambia has sparse, stunted forest growth, except in the valleys of its rivers, such as the Zambezi and the Kafue. On the Zambezi the huge Kariba Dam furnishes electrical power and irrigation to a large area on the border of Zimbabwe, the country which borders Zambia on the south.

Zambia has three seasons: cool and dry—May to July; warm and drier—August to October; hot and rainy—November to April. Malawi has only two seasons: May to October—dry; November to April—wet.

As one heads east into Malawi, the thin scrub changes to rolling green hills and forested mountains, with several lovely lakes. The largest, Lake Malawi, covers 8,000 square miles and is almost as large as Lake Huron in North America.

Zambia and Malawi cover an area almost as large as Ohio, Michigan, Indiana, Illinois, Wisconsin and Minnesota combined. But the population is only one-fourth that of these states.

The People

Although the populations of Zambia and Malawi are nearly the same, the latter, because of its smaller size, is more densely populated. The people of Zambia speak many dialects of Bantu origin, while the main language spoken in Malawi is Chewa.

183

Zambia's prosperity depends on copper; Malawi is largely agricultural. Cattle are raised in both countries, although the milk is not generally used and the meat only on special occasions. Many of the people have moved from the bush to the cities for more gainful employment, but farming is still the occupation of most of the population.

The people among whom our missionaries preach the gospel in the urban and rural areas have all come into contact with modern Western culture. A few of the people own cars, tractors and other modern tools. But bicycles are used everywhere because even the old foot paths can be negotiated with them. The bicycle is used by the men to get to work, for a family jaunt (it is not unusual to see a family of three on one bicycle) and for hauling purposes.

The African villages are interesting. Some consist of just a few huts thatched with elephant grass and built of wattle (upright poles interwoven with branches or vines) and daubed with a plaster of clay and manure. Bush villages are found throughout the countryside, located near good soil, firewood and water. Proximity to a flowing stream is also desirable, since fish constitute an important source of protein. Paths fan out in all directions from the villages through the tall elephant grass.

Natural Religion—Animism

"My forefathers knew about god and the spirits even before the Europeans (white men) came," Chief Shakumbila told the missionary as they talked together in his white frame house one November afternoon in 1961. He continued: "and when we wanted to pray to god we went to the graves of our 'old ones,' because then we did not know that God had sent his Son to speak to us."

It is true, the Africans had and still have a religion of their own. This is called animism because it is a worship of everything animate, such as trees, animals and birds, also of the spirits of those who have died and who are thought to be alive and haunting the living. The exercise of this religion consists chiefly in appeasing the evil spirits by certain superstitious practices and sacrifices and in consulting the witch doctors, who by their charms and chants ward off the spirits.

Evil spirits are thought to be the cause of every illness and every misfortune. This was shown clearly by the following account by one of our missionaries:

One night in November of 1961, the driver of our tractor at Lumano was fatally injured while towing the mission lorry, loaded with cement blocks. The lorry's brakes failed on a slight decline and the bumper of the lorry caught on the lugs of the tractor wheels, lifting the front end of the tractor and crushing the driver to death.

We reported the accident that same night to the wife of the stricken man. Hardly had we returned to the mission, when

184

Mr. Mulundika, the headmaster of the school, came to our window to tell us that the mother of the dead man had come to the mission with a group of her relatives to kill the driver of the lorry because his evil spirit was guilty of the accident. Fortunately, we had taken the precaution of taking the driver to the police post for protective custody only an hour earlier, and the mother and relatives were finally persuaded to go home.

However, a few days later the father of the dead man fled to our mission compound for protection from his wife for the same reason. He told us that his wife now believed his evil spirit caused the accident, because on the day of the accident the father had suddenly recovered from an illness. His evil spirit must have entered into the son and caused his death, and this had to be avenged by killing him. Such superstition is difficult to uproot; only faith in the loving Father of our Lord Jesus Christ can accomplish it through the Holy Spirit's power in the Word.

Chapter 37

LUTHERAN CHURCH OF CENTRAL AFRICA

Missionaries as "Medicine Men"

Invariably, the people to whom our missionaries bring the gospel of God's love in Christ Jesus will turn to the missionary to help them also in their physical suffering. Those who teach that Jesus had compassion on people and healed the sick (Matthew 14:14) will also be moved to compassion when they see people helpless and sick. Thus, the ministry to the sick has ever gone hand-in-hand with the preaching of the gospel. Our African people have always felt that they could come to the missionary or his wife for physical relief and simple medical aid. And they did come. Having replaced the medicine men as the spiritual leaders of the people, our missionaries also are looked upon as men of God who with their gifts and knowledge will heal people of their physical ills. At Lumano, informal treatment and dispensing activity increased until the missionary's wife, a trained nurse, was seeing over 500 patients at her front door during April 1960!

Our Medical Mission in Zambia

When reports of this situation reached our synodical congregations, faithful women responded generous-

Mwembezhi dispensary

ly. In 1957 the synod authorized an extra-budgetary medical mission project, headed by Arthur Tacke, M.D.

A 1960 survey, made by Mrs. Edgar Hoenecke, R.N., resulted in the decision to build a modest bush dispensary at Lumano on the Sala Reserve. It was to be staffed by one registered nurse and several African medical assistants who would be gradually trained to take over the operation themselves.

The Lumano Lutheran Dispensary was dedicated on November 26, 1961, and medical service was begun with nurse Barbara Welch in charge. In 1986, twenty-five years later, the renamed Mwembezhi (Shepherd) Lutheran Dispensary had two American

186

nurses and a case load of several thousand patients a month.

Expansion into Malawi in 1970

In Malawi the establishment of some type of medical service was required by the government if we were allowed to carry on mission work near the new capital, Lilongwe. At nearby Salima, on beautiful Lake Malawi, the government had cleared a swamp for a large agricultural development, staffed by farming experts from Germany. Here was our opportunity to open a mission near the new center of government, and we were able to acquire a large lake shore property which included a house for the missionary and his family, a home for a nurse, a guest home and servants' quarters, all furnished. A mobile medical clinic, serving at several loca-

Mobile clinic

tions, was set up in keeping with the government regulations under the supervision of nurse Edith Schneider. She had previously served in our Sala dispensary.

In time it became apparent that erosion was affecting the Salima lakeshore mission station; therefore, in 1984 the headquarters of the Malawi medical mission was transferred to Lilongwe. A mobile unit was then used to serve several clinics in both the Lilongwe and Salima areas.

Our Primary Purpose—the Gospel

Our medical dispensary program has always given our staff and the pastoral helpers an opportunity to tell the gospel truths to waiting patients. In this way, many have been led to find healing for their souls in Christ.

After all, it is not the prime purpose of our missions and missionaries to help people physically or socially. Our great, single purpose is to teach these people that they need not be slaves to their fear of evil spirits and foul witches, but that God has sent them a Savior who loves them, who died and rose for them and who will take them to himself in heaven when they die as believers in that Savior. It is our purpose to teach them the truth that will free them from fear of the devil and give them confidence, hope and joy which no man, no trouble, no evil spirit can ever take away from them. This is the assignment which was given to our first missionaries in 1953, and it is the same today.

Mission Work Prospers

The center of our African mission has been Lusaka, the capital of Zambia. In 1954 the request came from Chief Shakumbila to open missionary activity on the Sala Reserve, about forty miles west of Lusaka. With the mission our men were soon working

187

in two areas, the urban work in Lusaka and the work in the Bundu (bush) at Lumano. The work prospered. By 1957 six preaching places in Salaland were served, with weekly attendance of over 500. Classes for adults had begun. One hundred twenty boys and girls enrolled in our Martin Luther Boarding School at Lumano. Homes for our missionaries, modest schools and teachers' huts were built. Crops of maize, peanuts and sun-hemp were raised on mission allotment, and a sizable grove of banana, plaintain, orange, mango and papaya trees was set out.

"Sermon Boys"

A series of problems, reflecting the unrest in Africa at the time, disturbed the progress in the field from 1957 to 1960. Lack of staff made it impossible at times for our missionaries to cope with all the work in the many Sala villages. As an expedient, "Sermon Boys" from our Martin Luther school were sent out on bicycles to read the Sunday sermons to the villagers and to teach simple Bible stories to the children in the native dialects.

The work of the "Sermon Boys" was appreciated as a stop-gap, and it led to several of them volunteering to be trained for the ministry and, thus, to serious planning on our part to open a Bible Institute. However, at a meeting of twenty-one headmen we were asked to send our older men to preach because, as one village headman put it, "We do not listen to boys in our councils." A concerted effort was then made to secure older men for our missions in Central Africa. The combination of older and younger men has resulted in a well-balanced team of mission workers.

Preaching in the Native Language

The Board for World Missions insisted that the missionaries must learn the native language. This imposed a heavy, extra burden on the men, but, once the language had been learned, the preaching and teaching program was brought under the control of the missionaries. Since interpreters were no longer needed by the missionaries, the interest and response of the people improved dramatically.

Yet one must remember that there are over 800 languages and dialects in Africa and approximately seventy of these languages are spoken in Zambia alone. Among eleven students at our Bible Institute in 1966, eight different languages were represented. Even though we have missionaries who speak Chinyanja, Tonga, and Bemba, we could not carry on our instructions if the students did not learn English.

From the beginning our pastors have worked with African Christians to translate portions of the Bible, simple instruction courses, short meditations, prayers and hymns into the local language. These were then duplicated, and young men were sent out into the villages to read these portions to those who came.

Mailing Program Opens New Fields

A mailing program was also developed, and in a few years over 3,000 addresses were on the weekly mailing list.

Whenever a packet of Christian literature is sent to an address it does double duty. Not only is it read by the family receiving it, but neighbors and friends are invited to hear it read. These people have little opportunity to get hold of printed material, and when they do, they are vitally interested in learning what it says. In this way little groups of hearers gather regularly to hear the Word of God transmitted to them from the printed page. Many come to faith in their Savior by this simple means.

When questions are asked which cannot be answered from the material at hand, the people invariably ask the missionary to come more regularly or to send someone else to serve and instruct them. Many new fields have been opened in this way. The expansion of the mission in Malawi was the direct result of requests for resident missionaries by people who regularly gathered about the reading of the printed material sent through the mailing program.

A Gospel Singer and a 400-mile Bicycle Ride

Far more important for the African Christians than self-support and self-administration of their young church is the spiritual gift of giving expression to their faith, hope and joy in Christ in their own language. The Holy Spirit has given this gift to our young African church in rich measure.

Mr. Deverson Ntambo heard about Jesus Christ in his native Malawi from one of our missionaries. He left a good, white-collar position and enrolled in our Bible school at Lusaka. While he was there he began to write and sing songs of faith in the African style with his wife and children. One of his teachers wrote down the words and melodies which he composed, and today they are being sung in the African churches. One of these songs has been published and is being used by church choirs in our country.

Another young convert, Isaac K., a native of Zimbabwe, had come to Zambia in 1966 and found his Savior through our Lutheran mission. After his confirmation he remained at Lumano in Salaland to help the missionary by interpreting and instructing. One day he asked that he be permitted to go home to Zimbabwe, a round-trip by bicycle of over 400 miles, because, he said, "I have to tell my father and mother, my uncle, and my family about the wonderful things which I have found in Jesus Christ!"

A little over two weeks later he returned, overjoyed because his people had also come to believe in Jesus through his witnessing.

Native Helpers and a Tragic Death

Young Isaac is only one of many, young and old, who have gladly and faithfully helped our missionaries to overcome the language barrier and to witness for their Savior. The service of such faithful Christians is indispensable during the first difficult years before the missionaries have learned the native language, and they become more valuable as they grow more able to teach and to lead their people with their example of Christian faith and life.

But it is most important that they are also trained thoroughly in Christian doctrine, as well as in the practice set forth in Holy Scripture, if they are to lead in developing a true, Bible-centered Lutheran church.

A sad event must be recorded in the midst of all these good tidings. Dr. William Schweppe met with a fatal accident on July 15, 1968, on a narrow concrete strip road (two narrow concrete strips for the wheels) south of Lusaka, Zambia, as he was returning from one of the villages. The death of this experienced and beloved leader was deeply mourned by the Lutheran church of Central Africa.

Bible Institute and Seminary

One of the primary goals of all our world mission fields is to train witnesses, workers, and leaders from among the people to whom the Lord has sent us with his gospel. It is one thing for a pastor from the United States to learn to preach in a foreign language; it is quite another matter to train national pastors to proclaim the good news of the Savior to their own people in the mother tongue.

This training is done in the Zambia and Malawi Lutheran Bible Institutes and the Lutheran Seminary at Chelston near Lusaka. The seminary in Zambia supplies the fully-trained pastors for the church in both Zambia and Malawi.

The course for future pastors provides for two years in the Bible Institute and several years as pastoral helper in the field (under the supervision of a missionary), followed by

Seminary above Bible Institute left

three years at the seminary. A further two-year period as vicar ends in an oral and written examination. Those found qualified are ordained into the holy ministry as called pastors of the church. From the beginning of their ministerial training course the students are engaged in practical work, in making canvasses of villages, in teaching, in visiting the sick and delinquent, and in other assignments.

Building the Central African Church

The pastoral training program is an essential part of the growth, development and maturing of the national church. The goal of the program is to replace the American missionaries with national pastors as soon as possible without endangering the confessional orthodoxy of the young church. Eventually, the program should produce not only a national clergy, but also a staff of well-trained and competent national church leaders, both as administrators and as professors of theology who are "able to teach."

In keeping with this church policy and through the urging of our missionaries, the African congregations organized themselves as **The Lutheran Church of Central Africa** on September 7, 1965. Annual conventions of this church body have served to instruct and guide the members in assuming an ever greater responsibility for self-administration and self-support. Since 1972, conventions have been held every two years, just as in our synod.

Expansion—Malawi and Cameroon

When a number of families of our mission in Zambia moved to Malawi, our missionaries kept in contact with them by means of the monthly mailing program and one or two visits a year.

In response to urgent requests from these families in Malawi, Pastors R. Mueller and R. Cox conducted an extensive canvass in the area of Blantyre-Limbe. This led to the decision to send resident missionaries to Malawi in 1963. The work in Malawi has grown, and by 1980 it became our synod's largest mission in the number of people served. A Bible Institute for the training of evangelists was opened in Lilongwe in 1981.

Calls for aid have continued to come to our church from other parts of Africa. Since the middle of the 1970s our synod has provided the Lutheran Church of Cameroon (LCC) with financial assistance and spiritual guidance. The LCC carries on the Lord's work in the western African country of the United Republic of Cameroon.

The Tie That Binds— *"The Lutheran Christian"*

As the territory served by our mission grew, it became increasingly difficult to maintain contact and a sense of belonging between the far-flung mission outposts of the Lutheran Church of Central Africa (LCCA). Attendance by missionaries and delegates at conventions of the church and visits of men from the Lusaka headquarters were no longer enough.

The situation was greatly improved with the establishment of the Lutheran Press on the campus of the Bible Institute at Lusaka and the printing of uniformly good religious publications—in English, Chinyanja, Luvale and Tonga. The bi-monthly church paper, *The Lutheran Christian*, serves to tie the members of the LCCA together, especially since it appears in the four languages spoken by them and, in addition to the many doctrinal articles, brings news items from the various areas.

It is also interesting to note that for the second time in our synod's missionary history one of our missions has inspired a number of literary works. The first were the novels by Rev. J. F. Gustav Harders about Apaches in the early years of this century. The second are books written by former missionary and seminary professor, Ernst H. Wendland. He has written: *To Africa With Love, Of Other Gods and Other Spirits,* and *Dear Mr. Missionary.*

The Future in Africa

In Africa, as elsewhere, it is important that we work with zeal and faithfulness while the Lord still gives us the time and the opportunity. Our goal is to train qualified workers to take over the preaching and teaching of the Lutheran faith. The spirit of the national pastors who will carry on the work is expressed in verse by Mr. Deverson Ntambo:

Til' Ancito Ambuyeyo
(We are the Workers of the Lord)

We are the workers of the Lord.
Let us not falter in the work of His Word.
In the fight against Satan the Lord is our Help.
Chorus: The Lord says to us, why stand ye and wait?
To continue the work of the Word of the Lord;
This is the ladder to Heaven!

Unit Twelve

WORLD MISSIONS OF OUR CHURCH—PART 4

CHAPTERS

Chapter 38

LATIN AMERICAN MISSIONS

Beginning in Tucson

The "mother church" of our Latin American missions is the small San Pablo congregation in Tucson, Arizona. Forty years after it was first gathered, it was still listed as only a preaching station in the synod's *Statistical Report*. However, this is one of many instances where the true story of a mission can best be told, not in numbers gained but in the faith and perseverance of the missionary.

Rev. Venus Winter was already approaching middle age when he took up the study of Spanish while serving as pastor in Flint, Michigan. Shortly after this, he accepted a call to open a Spanish mission in Tucson. There was no nucleus of Spanish Lutherans to welcome him, but rather the opposite. When people heard that he was a follower of Dr. Luther, the "heretic," they said *No me gusta* (I don't like him). During the first year there were as many as sixteen consecutive Sundays when the only soul in church was the missionary himself. And this in spite of many house-to-house calls during the week. Yet the pastor's trust in God's promise: "[The] word that goes out from my mouth . . . will not return to me empty" (Isaiah 55:11) did not waver.

He wrote: "After nine months of calling on homes we [the missionary and his faithful daughter, Barbara—his wife having died before he came west] finally had a little Sunday school. This handful of children agreed to stay for church, and from that time on we had regular church services." The youthful congregation worshiped in rented quarters. For special classes they met in the adobe homes of the people who permitted their children to attend. When the missionary prepared for a Christmas program he would carry his portable organ to the homes of the children and rehearse the carols. "Our Christmas carols are especially beautiful in the melodious Spanish language," he said.

In 1949 early Sunday morning radio services in Spanish were begun. About 75 percent of the present members of San Pablo and of other Spanish speaking Lutheran groups in El Paso, Texas, and at Juarez, across the border in Mexico, were traceable to these broadcasts. A Spanish Lutheran elementary school opened in 1957. When the average Sunday church attendance reached between forty and fifty, the pastor rejoiced: "The Lord has done great things for us and we are filled with joy" (Psalm 126:3).

Two New Spanish Congregations

In 1967 the Spanish mission was expanded by two more congregations when Missionary Ernest Zimdars was called to El Paso, after having finished his Spanish language study at Saltillo, Mexico. During his stay at this school he met and married a young Mexican lady, who proved to be very helpful to him in his work, especially with the children at El Paso and Juarez. Small congregations were established in each of these cities, but it was difficult for an American pastor to serve in Mexico because of a Mexican law limiting pastoral activities to native-born Mexicans.

Our withdrawal from the Synodical Conference in 1963 was noted by many concerned Lutherans, including Dr. David Orea Luna, president of the Mexican Lutheran Church and professor of the Lutheran Seminary *"Augsburgo"* in Mexico City. For years he had been contending for orthodox Lutheran doctrine and practice against increasing liberal and unionistic tendencies in his own church, which was affiliated with the American Lutheran Church of our country. In 1964 he requested and received copies of our doctrinal and confessional writings from the president of our church.

Three years later, after constant, but ineffectual, efforts to lead his church back to confessional orthodoxy, Dr. Orea Luna and a young pastor (a former student of his) applied for an interview with men of our synod. The two Mexican pastors passed a formal colloquy, or examination, and were declared to be in fellowship with us. The young pastor was called to take charge of the Juarez congregation and of other small groups that had been won through the radio broadcasts.

Missioner Program in Puerto Rico

As early as 1960 the Board for World Missions had planned to penetrate into South America by way of Mexico but was thwarted by the Mexican law forbidding non-Mexican missionaries in that country. An alternate route had to be found. Because our supply of men and money was limited, the synod resolved to try a new way—really a very old and scriptural way—of doing mission work by initiating a Christian Missioner Corps program. Simply stated, this is a plan of sending missionaries into a new field to develop a church with the resources of the

El Piraquero (the snowcone maker);
Artist: Miquel Toro, Puerto Rico

195

people in the area, instead of building churches and supporting national workers with foreign funds. Like St. Paul, our missioners are expected to withdraw from the field as soon as the national church can take over.

After a preliminary survey, the Board for World Missions chose the little island of Puerto Rico to test the missioner corps program and to establish a bridgehead for work in South America. The population of the island is Spanish, but English is also spoken as the second language because Puerto Ricans consider themselves a part of the United States.

The work was begun there by Missionary Roger Sprain in 1964 in an impoverished area along a railroad spur leading into the sugar cane fields. It was called Gran Stan Bran (for Gran Stand Branch Station). A friendly but very outspoken lady, Dona Josepha, became one of the first converts and was a great help in gaining several others. When they were ready for a church, they bought an old shed for $145, paying $20 down and promising to retire the rest in monthly installments. After cleaning and whitewashing the building, they dedicated it with as much holy pride and joy as many others who build elaborate edifices.

But in 1973 the government relocated the people of that community to other areas of subsidized housing. The railroad spur was removed, the shacks were destroyed and the place reverted to grass and scrub trees. The chief crop of the island was switched from sugar cane to cotton. Neverthe-

Guayama Chapel, Puerto Rico

less the work continued. By 1985 three missioners and a vicar were active in Puerto Rico, serving several organized congregations and two preaching stations. Today work is also being carried on in Puerto Rico's capital, San Juan.

Mission in Colombia

Puerto Rico proved to be the bridge needed to begin work in South America. Two extensive surveys of mission potentials on that continent were made. The second one, lasting ten weeks, was conducted by two Spanish speaking pastors, Rupert Eggert of Puerto Rico and Ernest Zimdars of El Paso. They reported to the synodical convention in 1971, and on their recommendation the synod decided to open its mission in the city of Medellin (meh-deh-YEEN), Colombia. Two years passed before three missioners—two pastors, Roger Sprain and Ernest Zimdars, and one teacher, Francis Warner—were called. They were commissioned on August 14, 1973, in the closing service of that year's synodical convention.

Medellin, Colombia

The three men, two experienced in mission work and all capable of speaking Spanish, arrived in Medellin during January 1974. After finding rented homes for their families, they held the first public service on the first Sunday in February. Five people were present, but that number soon increased to an average of fifty each Sunday. Services were held in the Warner residence, and later when the Sprains moved into a larger house, in the Sprain residence. In 1975 this congregation bought a house that could serve as a chapel and took the name of Santa Trinidad. At that time it was one of three established congregations in Medellin and its suburbs.

There were also two preaching stations, at Envigado and Mirimar. The one at Envigado seemed to hold the promise of becoming another thriving congregation, but here for the first time the opposition of a Catholic priest, who lived across the street, hampered the work.

The missioners met regularly to study and to plan courses of instruction for Colombians at all levels—confirmands, Sunday school teachers, congregational leaders and future pastors. The missioners also initiated a regular radio program and established a seminary and Bible institute, following the model of the one in Zambia.

In 1985 a new church building was dedicated in downtown Medellin, thereby providing a more centrally located place for holding services. Two years before that, in 1983, the Colom-

197

Most Holy Trinity, Medellin, Colombia

bian Lutheran Church ordained its first national pastor, Omar Ortiz. This enabled the missioners to extend their work into Bogota, Colombia's capital city. Since that time Pastor Ortiz resigned his office, but the work continues in both Medellin and Bogota.

Lutheran Churches in Mexico

When the bond of fellowship was declared between two Mexican pastors and our synod in 1967, it meant that Dr. Orea Luna lost his offices as president and professor of the Lutheran Seminary in Mexico City. About sixty members of his congregation remained loyal to Scripture and to him, although this meant losing the church building in which they had been worshiping. They were not able to gather for worship until two years later, when their new church was dedicated. Mexican law prevented the congregation from renting a place for worship. The rented building would have been "nationalized"—that is, taken over by the government. No owner would risk this with his property.

During the many months while they were without a church, the pastor held regular family devotions for each of his members in their homes and succeeded in keeping his little flock almost intact. After much discouragement and delay, a beautiful little church was built. The congregation furnished the interior, and our synod paid for the building. When it was completed it was turned over to the Mexican government, which in turn assigned it for church use to the congregation.

Dr. Orea Luna began instructing several theological students at a study center connected with the church. He also published a Spanish church paper, which he called *El Amanecer* (The Dawning). When this gifted man died unexpectedly in 1972, his students continued their training in a seminary established by our synod in El Paso, Texas. This El Paso seminary plans to serve students from Colombia, Mexico and Puerto Rico who desire to enter the ministry. At present, we have congregations in Mexico City, Puebla, Monterrey, Guadalajara and Juarez. They are served primarily by four national pastors.

Church service in Guadalajara, Mexico

198

ORTHODOX LUTHERAN CHURCH OF BRAZIL

Contacts from Brazil, the largest of the South American countries, began in 1975. Senor Luiz Rauter, who was concerned about the drifting away from pure scriptural doctrine in the Lutheran church to which he belonged, started a small church near the southern coastal town of Porto Alegre. It was called the Brazil Lutheran Orthodox Church. Soon others joined with him in worshiping the Lord in Gravatai. Senor Rauter was not the only one to contact our synod for workers. Dr. Paul Oserow, a practicing attorney in Dourados and former Lutheran pastor, also appealed for workers from our synod.

During its 1985 convention, our synod authorized the sending of an exploratory team to Brazil. Two years later the synod convention received a favorable report from the team. As a result, our synod approved the sending of five missionaries to Brazil. Members of the synod showed their eagerness to underwrite the costs by contributing special gifts which totaled nearly $500,000 by 1988.

The first missionary to accept a call was Pastor Charles Flunker, who had served in Puerto Rico for 13 years. During October 1987 two others joined him in Porto Alegre. They were Pastor Richard Starr, who was called to serve as the mission coordinator, and Pastor Bruce Marggraf. Their first major assignment was to learn the Portuguese language. Our Brazil mission team became complete when Pastor Charles Gumm accepted a call and seminary candidate Kenneth Cherney was assigned to this field, both in 1988.

Chapter 39

EUROPEAN MISSIONS

"Polish" Mission

More than twenty years ago any history of the Wisconsin Synod still included a chapter on our missions in Germany. Today these mission churches are no longer in fellowship with us, though a few slender threads still tie us by way of correspondence to a Lutheran church in East Germany (the German Democratic Republic). What follows is a brief historical summary of attempts made during the last sixty years to establish and maintain a confessional Lutheran church in the land of the Reformation.

Our missionary work began in Poland in 1924. The Polish people themselves are Roman Catholic, but there were large colonies of German Lutherans in the new Polish republic established by the victorious Allies after World War I. These people were allowed to have their own Lutheran organization, called the Augsburg Church, a unionistic state church. A small group of confessional Lutherans under a Pastor Angerstein of the city of Lodz tried to preserve the orthodox Lutheran faith by sending seminarians to our Wisconsin Lutheran Seminary, and this was the first link between the Wisconsin Synod and Lutherans in Poland.

At the request of two large congregations in Poland, we sent one of our pastors, Otto Engel, to supervise the founding of a true Lutheran church in that country. It was our first mission on foreign soil and the second in a foreign language—the Apache being the first. Though there was intense opposition both from the Augsburg Church and the Polish government, our mission managed to survive. Before World War II it had grown from thirty-five to 1,800 communicants. The resident superintendent was one of our pastors, William Bodamer.

Refugee Missions

The Second World War brought an end to our Polish mission. When the news of what happened finally reached this country, it was sad indeed. The policy not only of the Russians and Poles but also of the retreating German army was to drive all German people out of Poland. Often at gunpoint they were forced to leave their homes and all their possessions. Arriving in Germany the refugees found a cold welcome because the country was already overcrowded with impoverished people who had lost everything in the great defeat.

The congregations had been broken up and separated from their pastors.

Yet six of the pastors managed to get together in the German city of Zwickau. From there they plodded on foot from place to place until they rounded up a remnant of their people and founded the Refugee Mission Church. In West Germany that soon developed into the Church of the Ev. Lutheran Confession. The refugees in East Germany became a district of the Saxon Lutheran Free Church. Their lot was worse because of harassment from the Communist government.

Yet our refugee churches grew soon after the war until we were serving over 17,000 members. Many of them were probably more interested in the gifts of food, clothing and Care packages than in Lutheran doctrines, however, for twenty years later the number of active members had dwindled to 3,000. Religious indifference, growing material prosperity and the pressure to join the state churches all played a part in the final parting of the ways. It was unionism—affiliating or maintaining friendly relations with the more liberal West German evangelical church and the Lutheran Church-Missouri Synod—that led at last to the suspensions of fellowship with our former mission churches and also with the Lutheran church of France and Belgium. The two pastors from our church presently in Germany are not missionaries in the usual sense, but chaplains to our members serving in the American armed forces in western Europe.

Lutheran Confessional Church in Scandinavia

An altogether more heartening experience took place in Sweden, where a small group of confessional pastors and people dissolved their connections with the unorthodox Swedish Lutheran state church and established contact with our church. The leading pastor in Sweden was Dr. Seth Erlandsson. Our contact man was Dr. Siegbert W. Becker of our Wisconsin Lutheran Seminary.

THE LUTHERAN CONFESSIONAL CHURCH (SCANDINAVIA)

This map shows the location of the congregations that make up the LCC

• Congregations

The first confessional Swedish Lutheran Church was formed in 1973, and the Lutheran Confessional Church (LCC) of Sweden, Norway and Finland was organized in Sweden a year later. By 1985 the LCC had

201

grown to eight congregations in Sweden, three in Norway and several preaching stations in Finland. These congregations and stations were served by 16 pastors. In 1987, however, several pastors and some members broke from this fellowship because of doctrinal disagreement. The Lutheran Confessional Church trains its future church workers in a school in Upsala, Sweden, called the Bible Research Institute Biblicum. Here materials have been prepared in the form of tracts, cassettes and pamphlets which are widely distributed in the Scandinavian countries to acquaint interested people with conservative Lutheran teachings.

The LCC is in fellowship with our synod, which granted a onetime gift of $50,000 as a nucleus for a Swedish church extension fund. Other financial support is made possible entirely by generous gifts from members of our church. No synodical budgetary funds are involved. The members of the LCC contribute substantially to the work of their church. The assistance our members provide is the margin which makes it possible for the work to move forward.

Chapter 40

IN CONCLUSION

Our Mission

When one considers that our synod's present world missions—except for those in Apacheland—were begun as recently as the early 1950s, the scope of the work today is truly amazing. Equally impressive is the spirit of all those connected with it—the dedication of the many missionaries who bear the brunt of the work in the mission fields (and we should not forget their families); the enthusiasm of the various boards, committees, chairmen and administrators who plan and direct the work; and the generosity of our synod's members whose gifts make the work possible. Many of our members donate sums for special purposes apart from their regular contributions to the synodical treasury. The mission in Colombia, which was decided in 1971 but then postponed because of a shortage of funds, could not have been opened even in 1973 had it not been for the gift of $144,000 from a single family for that purpose. Similarly, gifts of hundreds of thousands of dollars have made possible the beginning in southern Brazil.

Mission work and everything connected with it is essentially a labor of love, of bringing the gospel to others as it was once brought by missionaries to our forefathers. Christians are and must be a light in the world. This wonderful privilege of giving light to darkened souls is worth all the costs of the missions and all the hardships and trials in the mission fields. It is in this way that our Savior wants us to carry out his Great Commission (Matthew 28:18-20). It was the Great Commission of our risen Lord that began the story of World Missions.

Our Heritage

This story of *OUR CHURCH: Its Life and Mission* has taken the reader a long way—from the homes of our ancestors in the towns and villages of 19th century Germany, across the Atlantic Ocean to the eastern shores of the United States and from there to a forested new land called Wisconsin.

Here the Lutheran pioneers established their homes on farms and in towns. They founded congregations, called pastors and teachers, and built churches and parish schools. They enjoyed the good life in a country that provided them with material blessings and guaranteed them freedom to worship their Lord according to their consciences, to teach their faith to their children and to seek to win converts through missionary work.

After several decades Wisconsin Lutherans joined those of neighboring states in a federation, first with Minnesota and Michigan, then in a joint synod with additional states—Nebraska, the Dakotas, Montana and Washington. Rather early in the story, the first "foreign" mission was opened in Arizona among the Apache Indians. More recently, our church extended its activities at home and abroad so that it is now represented by congregations or missions in all states of the Union, in three Canadian provinces and in fifteen other countries on five continents.

Spiritually, the reader traveled another long way—from the mild Lutheranism of our founders to the strictly confessional, doctrinally oriented church that we are today. The theological road was not always smooth. Differences over matters of doctrine and church practice sometimes led to suspensions of fellowship and the parting of friends. Our church also passed through financial depressions that hindered its work and once or twice even raised doubts as to whether it would survive.

On one such occasion, during the Great Depression of the 1930s, when there were proposals to merge all the synods of the Synodical Conference, our Conference of Presidents delivered the following opinion: "Amalgamation would mean disbanding the Wisconsin Synod, something that would sadden us deeply. For our Synod has become very dear to us and has a deep meaning for us. It has its own history and has gone through some fiery struggles for the truth."

The last two sentences of this statement, uttered more than a generation ago, might almost serve as a summary of the present book, for it relates the history of this very synod, which became dear and meaningful to its members because it always proclaimed, maintained and in fiery struggles fought for the truth of the gospel as it is revealed in the Word of God.

INDEX